MICKEY ROGERS
JOANNE TAYLORE-KNOWLES
STEVE TAYLORE-KNOWLES

# SPEAK YOUR MIND

**STUDENT'S BOOK**
+ access to Student's App, Digital
Student's Book and Digital Workbook

## 5A

| | Outcomes | Vocabulary | Grammar | Speaking |
|---|---|---|---|---|
| **Unit 1**<br>Glocal<br>pp. 8–19<br>▶ | • Share your ideas on local and global businesses<br>• Talk about finance and cryptocurrencies<br>• Make arguments for and against global trade | • Trade<br>• Phrasal verbs<br>• Finance vocabulary | • Review of perfect forms<br>• Articles | • Discuss the origins of products<br>• Share your ideas about governments and local businesses |
| | | | Grammar Reference<br>pp. 156–157 | Speaking Practice<br>p. 148 |
| | Life Skills—Inquiry | | | |
| **Unit 2**<br>Sports Update<br>pp. 20–31<br>▶ | • Discuss ways to change sports<br>• Talk about technology and sports<br>• Talk about sports management | • Nouns and verbs with the same form<br>• Business and economics<br>• Adjectives and adverb collocations | • Verb + gerund<br>• Relative pronouns with –ever and no matter | • Compare your ideas on biomechanics<br>• Discuss the different statements about sports |
| | | | Grammar Reference<br>pp. 158–159 | Speaking Practice<br>p. 148 |
| | Life Skills—Equality | | | |
| **Unit 3**<br>Medicine on the Mend<br>pp. 32–43<br>▶ | • Discuss medical services<br>• Talk about technology in medicine<br>• Compare different medical beliefs | • Dependent prepositions<br>• Medical terms<br>• Verbs of thought | • Mixed conditionals<br>• Clauses of contrast and purpose | • Compare your ideas about a newspaper story<br>• Discuss ideas for the competition |
| | | | Grammar Reference<br>pp. 160–161 | Speaking Practice<br>p. 149 |
| | Life Skills—Critical literacy | | | |
| **Unit 4**<br>The World We Build<br>pp. 44–55<br>▶ | • Ask and answer questions about planned communities<br>• Share ideas on sustainable architecture<br>• Talk about the importance of sustainable design | • Urban areas<br>• Sustainable architecture<br>• Verb prefixes dis–, out–, and un– | • Inverted conditionals<br>• Review of adverbs | • Discuss the pros and cons of a planned community<br>• Talk about your plans for sustainable buildings |
| | | | Grammar Reference<br>pp. 162–163 | Speaking Practice<br>p. 149 |
| | Life Skills—Decision-making | | | |
| **Unit 5**<br>Our Changing Future<br>pp. 56–67<br>▶ | • Make predictions about the future<br>• Brainstorm solutions to future global issues<br>• Talk about changes in population trends | • Progress<br>• Adverbs of attitude<br>• Verb + noun + infinitive | • Future perfect<br>• Future perfect progressive | • Share your future predictions<br>• Discuss predictions of daily life in the year 3000 |
| | | | Grammar Reference<br>pp. 164–165 | Speaking Practice<br>p. 150 |
| | Life Skills—Global competence | | | |

| Pronunciation | Reading | Listening | Writing | Thinking Skill | Confident Communicator |
|---|---|---|---|---|---|
| • Stress in compound nouns | Read a blog post about finance<br>• Skill—Recognize the purpose and audience | Listen to a conversation about global and local businesses<br>• Skill—Listen for reasons and explanations | Write a report | Summarizing | Working effectively in a group |

| Pronunciation | Reading | Listening | Writing | Thinking Skill | Confident Communicator |
|---|---|---|---|---|---|
| • Nouns and verbs with the same form | Read an article about ways to improve sports<br>• Skill—Identify opinions | Listen to a conversation about the Olympics<br>• Skill—Understand attitude | Write a summary using a survey | Deducing | Translating for informal communication |

| Pronunciation | Reading | Listening | Writing | Thinking Skill | Confident Communicator |
|---|---|---|---|---|---|
| • Silent letters | Read an article about medical services<br>• Skill—Predict content using visuals | Listen to a radio show about technological innovations in medicine<br>• Skill—Use context clues to infer meaning | Write a blog post about medical tech | Analyzing | Communicating between cultures |

| Pronunciation | Reading | Listening | Writing | Thinking Skill | Confident Communicator |
|---|---|---|---|---|---|
| • /ʌ/, /ʊ/, and /uː/ | Read a poster for a competition<br>• Skill—Identify reasons | Listen to an interview<br>• Skill—Listen for agreement and disagreement | Write an email proposal | Symbolizing | Simplifying information |

| Pronunciation | Reading | Listening | Writing | Thinking Skill | Confident Communicator |
|---|---|---|---|---|---|
| • Adverbs of attitude | Read an opinion about inventions<br>• Skill—Identify main ideas | Listen to a science podcast about future resources<br>• Skill—Understand reference | Write an opinion post about future world problems | Brainstorming | Adapting language |

# Grammar Quiz: What Do You Already Know?

**A Choose the correct option.**

**1** My new school has strict rules. We **are encouraged to wear** / **are required to wear** uniforms. If we don't, they send us home. And they **don't let us use** / **don't make us use** our phones in class.

**2** I got a new phone number. My phone rang, and I didn't recognize the caller ID. It **might have been** / **couldn't have been** a friend because my friends don't have my new number. It **must have been** / **may not have been** a wrong number.

**3** Todd and I were surprised Delia came to the party because we didn't invite her. Todd **might have told** / **couldn't have told** her about it. She **mustn't have heard** / **may have heard** about it from Ellen.

**4** My new job is great. I **have to ask** / **am encouraged to ask** questions in meetings if I don't understand something. And my boss says I **can work** / **shouldn't work** from home if I want.

**B Complete the paragraph with the infinitive or gerund form of the verb in parentheses.**

Dying jobs are jobs that were popular but are not common anymore. One example is film developer. If you are over a certain age, you might remember **1** _____ (buy) film for your camera and going to a store **2** _____ (get) the film developed into prints. Fewer people use cameras with film now, as most people enjoy **3** _____ (take) photos with their phones. Now that **4** _____ (develop) film into prints is not popular, there are very few film developers. Another example is the postal worker. Instead of **5** _____ (send) letters, today people send email or texts. Technology is also reducing the number of taxi drivers. Ride share apps allow you **6** _____ (avoid) taking a taxi. Another example is video store owner. If you would like **7** _____ (see) a movie, you definitely don't need **8** _____ (go) to the local video store. You just download or stream the movie.

**C Unscramble the words to make sentences.**

**1** what's / of us / know / we / expected / all
_____.

**2** with her / a good boss / she's / as long as / you / agree
_____.

**3** mistakes / your essay / there are / check / in case
_____.

**4** you / important / to work / what / wear / isn't
_____.

**5** had known / would have been / if / he / he / here
_____.

**6** you / if / study / a good grade / hard / you / will get
_____.

**D** Complete the sentences with the words from the box.

> do   each   higher   large   little   more and more

1 I don't have a tablet computer, but I _____ have a laptop computer.
2 I like how _____ person in the photo is wearing a different color.
3 The bigger the budget, the _____ the risk to the movie studio.
4 Please hurry and get ready as we have _____ time.
5 I found a _____, pink necklace in my mother's jewelry box.
6 It seems like _____ people are streaming movies these days.

**E** Read the email. Choose the correct option.

| New Message | |
|---|---|
| To: Megan | Cc   Bcc |
| Subject: A crazy week | |

Megan-

This **1 has been / has been being** a crazy week. Yesterday, I **2 was giving / was supposed to give** a presentation at work, but I ended up calling in sick. People from our Mexico City office **3 were coming / will be coming** in the afternoon, and I think I just got nervous. I ended up giving the presentation today, and it was fine. But yesterday I felt bad because I told my team I **4 will be / would be** there.

Anyway, I **5 was going to write / will be written** to you last week, but I didn't have time. I want to go over my arrival plans for next week. I **6 was going to come / will be coming** in on Flight 504 next Saturday at 12:30 p.m. Can you pick me up? I **7 wouldn't check / won't be checking** any baggage, so I should be in the arrival area soon after the plane lands. All my projects at work **8 will be doing / will be done** by Friday, so I can really relax and we can enjoy ourselves. I can't wait to catch up!

Caitlyn

Send

**F** Find one error in each sentence. Write the correct sentence.

1 The Farm Market Café, that uses only organic ingredients, has a great menu.

_____.

2 He booked the tour with my cousin Jerry who's a travel agent.

_____.

3 I don't prefer to sit next to the window.

_____.

4 He asked me Haley would be at the meeting.

_____.

5 Would you rather leaving now or a little later?

_____?

6 The server had already been starting to take my order when I realized I had forgotten my wallet.

_____.

Go to the Grammar Review on pages 154–155.

## WHAT DO YOU ALREADY KNOW?

**1 IN GROUPS** Think about the stores you and your family go to. Discuss which factors most influence your decision to buy a product—the price, the quality, the country of origin, the popularity of the product, or something else.

## THINK AND PREPARE

**2** Decide whether you agree or disagree with this statement.

*We should only use products that are made in our own country.*

**3 IN GROUPS** Prepare for a speech where you will present your ideas about using a variety of products from different cultures and countries. Make notes on your position and reasons. Consider these points:
- where the products in the stores around you come from
- how important variety is to you
- whether you think imported products are good or bad for your country's economy

**VIDEO**

Watch the video as you prepare to give a speech and find out how to organize your ideas.

## SPEAK YOUR MIND

**4** Give your speech. Try to persuade others to your point of view.

## In this unit, you will ...

- discuss the origins of products and share your ideas on the role of local businesses.
- focus on Mediation: work effectively in a group.
- focus on a Thinking Skill: summarizing.
- read about how trade influences cultures.
- learn about inquiry: use questions to find out more about cryptocurrencies.
- practice your oral exam skills by having a two-way discussion.

## READING

**A IN PAIRS** Write the name of the country where you think each food comes from under the image. Then check the answers with your teacher. Do the origins of the foods surprise you?

**B IN PAIRS READING SKILL—Recognize purpose and audience** Read the text and discuss the questions.

1 What type of text is this? Why did the author write it?
2 Who is it aimed at?

**C** 🔊 **1.01** Read the text again. Then answer the questions.

## Finance Watch

| Home | Search | Archives | Contact | About Me |

### What I Learned From My Lunch
September 28

Today, my fellow watchers, my worldview changed over lunch, and I wanted to share it with you. I was in a local Italian restaurant, enjoying a delicious pasta dish, when my friend explained that pasta is not actually Italian, but Chinese! Later, I did a little investigation about pasta, and while my friend wasn't exactly right, it made me think a lot about the history of trade and the recent debates about the importance of international **trade policies**.

The popular story is that when the explorer Marco Polo, from Venice, returned from his exploration of China in 1292, he **imported** pasta to Italy. However, there is a historical document in the Spaghetti Museum in Pontedassio, Italy, from 1279 describing a soldier leaving pasta for his family. Clearly, pasta had existed in Italy long before Marco Polo returned to Venice.

Pasta may have arrived in Italy from a number of different sources. One possible source was Chinese **tradespeople** selling pasta to the Italians. There is a long history of pasta in China, including historical evidence from 300 BCE of Chinese writings about noodles. Another possible explanation is that pasta was **exported** from the Middle East to Italy. The Italians could have **purchased** pasta from the Persians (now the Iranians) in the Middle East. *Reshteh* is the word for "string" in the Iranian language of Farsi, and Persians have cooked *reshteh* since the medieval period. But is the origin of pasta really that important? Arguably, Italians are now the pasta experts because they have been creating classic pasta recipes for close to a thousand years. And it made me think about how international trade can really benefit a country.

In the week before my eye-opening pasta lunch, there were several debates in the news about restrictions on international trade. For several months, representatives of different groups had been arguing the advantages and disadvantages of **free trade**. After learning about how trade benefited and changed pasta, I now understand the argument for not limiting the number of countries we trade with. I believe we should remove all **trade barriers** and allow other countries to both freely sell us products and buy our products. Every **business enterprise** today knows the importance of different perspectives. Pasta is an excellent example of this. Because of trade, influences from multiple countries helped pasta become the world-famous food it is today. Why not allow this to happen for all types of products?

---

**GLOSSARY**

**BCE (phrase):** Before Common Era, to indicate a date that was before year 1 of the modern calendar
**eye-opening (adj):** making you feel surprised about something you learn

1 What did the writer's lunch help her learn?
2 Who do people commonly believe was responsible for bringing pasta to Italy?
3 Which other cultures does the writer say may have introduced pasta to Italy?
4 What argument is the author making about trade?
5 How does the history of the pasta trade help support her argument?

## VOCABULARY trade

**A** Match the words in bold in READING **C** to the definitions (1–8).

1 _____: people who sell products or services
2 _____: restrictions on free international exchange of products or services
3 _____: laws controlling the international exchange of products or services
4 _____: a system with low or no taxes on international products
5 _____: to buy something
6 _____: an organization that buys or sells products or services for money
7 _____: to buy and bring in a product from another country
8 _____: to sell and send products to another country

 **MAKE IT YOURS**

What products does your country import from other countries? What does your country export? What other types of trading do you know of? Look up other types of trading and the words related to trading.

## PRONUNCIATION stress in compound nouns

**A** 🔊 1.02 Listen to the compound nouns from VOCABULARY **A**. Underline the word that is stressed.

business enterprise   free trade   trade barrier   tradespeople   trade policy

**B** IN PAIRS Practice saying the compound nouns with the correct stress. Work with your partner to think of other compound nouns with *business*.

## GRAMMAR review of perfect forms

**A** Match the underlined parts of the excerpts from READING **C** to the perfect tenses.

1 present perfect: a situation that began in the past and is still true
2 past perfect: a situation or event that happened before another event in the past
3 present perfect progressive: emphasizes that an action started in the past and continued until another event happened
4 past perfect progressive: an action that continued until another event happened

a Clearly, pasta <u>had existed</u> in Italy long before Marco Polo returned to Venice. __2__
b Persians <u>have cooked</u> *reshteh* since the medieval period. __1__
c For several months, representatives of different groups <u>had been arguing</u> the advantages and disadvantages of free trade. __4__
d They <u>have been creating</u> classic pasta recipes for close to a thousand years. __3__

For more practice, go to page 156.

**B** IN PAIRS Discuss the questions about the examples in A.

1 In example **a**, which of the two actions happened first in history? What tense is used to describe that action? *past perf.*
2 In example **b**, why does the writer use the present perfect?
3 In example **c**, what tense is used to describe an action that began before another event in the past and continued?
4 In example **d**, why is the present perfect progressive used? *emphasize the time*

**C** Complete the sentences with the appropriate perfect tenses. Use negatives when necessary.

1 The evidence shows that Italians _had been eating_ (eat) pasta for 20 years before Marco Polo returned to Venice.

2 In recent years, many countries _had been discussing_ (discuss) changes to international trade.

3 Mexico _has been exporting_ (export) cacao for making chocolate for hundreds of years.

4 Even though the government _hadn't made_ (make) a decision yet, the foreign representatives asked for an answer on the trade agreement.

5 I _have_ always _liked_ (like) learning about new perspectives on popular history.

**D** **IN PAIRS** Discuss the questions. Then share your ideas with the class.

1 What foods have people been cooking for hundreds of years in your country?

2 Are there any new foods you or your family hadn't eaten before they were sold in your area?

## SPEAKING

For more speaking practice, go to page 148.

**A** Take the quiz to see how much you know about the origins of common products. Then check the answers with your teacher.

# Where in the World Did These Foods Come From?

1. coffee
   - a Ethiopia
   - b Italy
   - c Colombia

2. pineapples
   - a Hawaii
   - b Brazil and Paraguay
   - c Indonesia

3. turkeys
   - a the Americas
   - b Europe
   - c Asia

4. oranges
   - a the USA
   - b China and India
   - c Spain

5. apples
   - a Central Europe
   - b Africa
   - c Central Asia

6. tomatoes
   - a Asia
   - b Europe
   - c the Americas

**B** **IN GROUPS** Discuss the questions.

1 Which facts about the origins of the products in the quiz surprised you? Where had you thought those products originated?

2 Which of the products in the quiz does your country produce? Historically, have these products been mainly used in your country, or have they been exported to other countries?

## LISTENING

**A** **IN PAIRS** Look at the products below and list as many companies as you can that produce these products.

asics
nike
adidas
puma
mizuno

invicta
citizen
casio
apple
Rolex

frank and ferd
Dominos
Pizza hot
Soho
Papa Jonh

Paco Rabane
Dior
Calvin Klein
Gap
Ralph laurn

Kibon
Haug Daz
Cold Stop
Ban el Jerrys

Lavis
GAP
american eagle
calvin klein
wrangler

**B** Look at your lists and answer the questions.

1 How many of the companies on your lists are global?
2 How many of them are local?
3 What do the lists tell you about where your products normally come from?

*A: I think most of the companies on my list are global.*
*B: One of mine is a local company. I usually buy pizzas from the pizza place near my house.*

**C** 🔊 **1.03** Listen to two people talking about the effects that global businesses had on their local businesses. Underline the phrases they use to introduce a reason or an explanation.

however **owing to** given that **therefore** due to
**on the other hand** **for example**
**because of** **according to**

**D** 🔊 **1.03 LISTENING SKILL—Listen for reasons and explanations** Listen again to each speaker. Write the reasons for each speaker's actions in your notebook.

1 Why did the man move back to Mexico City?
2 Why did the man have to run the business by himself?
3 How did other companies affect the man's business?
4 How did the woman's business become successful?
5 Why did the bank move its head office out of the city?
6 What main reason does the woman give for why her profits have increased?

> 💡 **MAKE IT REAL**
>
> *That's why* is often used to introduce a reason in spoken English, e.g., *That's why I was left to do everything on my own.*

**GLOSSARY**

**booming (adj):** experiencing a period of economic success
**to corner the market (idiom):** to be more successful than any other company at selling a particular product

**E** **IN PAIRS** Discuss the questions.

1 Would you prefer to work for a global or a local business? Why?
2 What challenges, if any, do you think local businesses in your area face?

## VOCABULARY phrasal verbs

**A** Look at these sentences from LISTENING C. Choose the meaning of the underlined phrasal verb.

**1** The Hostel Roma <u>closed down</u> in 2017.
**a** stopped operating as a business
**b** shut for a short period of time

**2** Then I got a call from the National Food Truck Association, which is an organization I <u>belong to</u>.
**a** am a member of
**b** am owned by

**3** It was <u>putting me off</u> running the business, to be honest …
**a** making me want to continue
**b** making me want to stop

**4** Then the person I thought was my friend <u>backed out</u> and went to Europe with his girlfriend.
**a** decided not to do something he'd agreed to
**b** had an accident

**5** Because I've cornered the market in Thai food, I'm guaranteed to <u>sell out</u> by the end of the day …
**a** have nothing left to sell
**b** have lots left to sell

**6** I think it's true to say that my small business <u>took off</u> due to help … from a multinational bank.
**a** became international
**b** became successful

**7** In the first couple of years, we did really well, and things started to <u>look up</u>.
**a** get worse
**b** get better

**8** It was always my intention to <u>start up</u> my own business …
**a** control
**b** establish

**B** **IN PAIRS** Discuss what local business you would choose to start up and why. How would you compete with global businesses?

## GRAMMAR articles

**A** Read these grammar rules about articles. Match the rules (a–j) to the examples from LISTENING C (1–10).

We use *a/an* (the indefinite article) …
**a** to talk about one of many things.
**b** when we talk about something for the first time.
We use *the* (the definite article) …
**c** when it's clear which thing(s) we're talking about, often because we've mentioned the thing(s) before.
**d** with superlative forms.
**e** with the names of rivers, seas, oceans, mountain ranges, deserts, plural country names, and island groups.
**f** with the names of hotels, most movie theaters, and most museums and art galleries.

We use no article (the zero article) …
**g** with a plural noun.
**h** with uncountable nouns.
**i** with the names of most countries, continents, states, mountains, and lakes.
**j** with towns, cities, neighborhoods, and streets.

*more work*

For more practice, go to page 157.

**1** … I convinced my family to give me **money** … ___ *a*
**2** I decided to move back to **Mexico City** … ___ *the*
**3** I was able to buy **an old building** … _____
**4** It was **the most amazing** opportunity … _____
**5** I was living in the **US** … _____
**6** **The Hostel Roma** closed down in 2017. _____
**7** I had **a friend** I'd known since we were young, and he and I agreed to go into business together. _____
**8** … and went to **Europe** with his girlfriend. _____
**9** We thought it would appeal to **experienced travelers**. _____
**10** Somehow, I managed to get **the hostel** opened in 2012. _____

**B** Check (✓) the correct sentences. Rewrite the incorrect sentences in your notebook.

1 ☐ My neighborhood has best Thai restaurants.
2 ☐ It seems that all towns have similar businesses no matter where they are.
3 ☐ I'm going to the local museum of modern art later. Do you want to come?
4 ☐ In New York, Hudson River provides water for many local businesses.
5 ☐ Jenny is accountant for a large insurance company.
6 ☐ After reviewing her proposal, the bank manager gave Sara a small business loan.

**C** **IN PAIRS** Discuss the questions.

1 What is an example of a great local business in your city or town?
2 What are the positive and negative effects of global trade on local businesses?

## WRITING a report

**A** Read this report about different cafés in a local area. What does the report specifically look at?

### Cafés in the Downtown Area

**Introduction**
This report on the cafés operating in the downtown area looks at how they serve the needs of consumers and ways for the government to support local businesses.

**Global Businesses**
There are three branches of Coffeebean Café and two branches of Colombia Coffeehouse. These are popular with businesspeople working in the nearby offices. Both cafés are open until 10 p.m. The customers believed that they offer good value for money and the prices were reasonable, but the quality varied between branches.

**local businesses**
there are two other cafés in the downtown area the historic café de paris and the italian café in victoria square both of these are popular with tourists and local people both cafés close at six and that is earlier than other businesses customers reported that the service was excellent but the prices were high they felt that the overall quality was good

**Conclusion**
These cafés are popular with different groups of people, so there is little direct competition between them. However, local businesses would benefit from longer opening hours. Perhaps the government could support the local cafés by offering discounted rents. This would help the businesses afford to pay for more employees so that they could stay open later.

**B** Match the punctuation (1–9) to the correct symbol (a–i).

1 exclamation mark __e__
2 comma __a__
3 colon __c__
4 period __b__
5 quotation marks __f__
6 question mark __i__
7 semicolon __d__
8 hyphen __h__
9 apostrophe __g__

a ,
b .
c :
d ;
e !

f " "
g '
h -
i ?

**C** **IN PAIRS** Correct the punctuation and capitalization mistakes in the paragraph about local businesses in **A**. There are 20 in total. Compare your answers with a partner.

## SPEAKING

For more speaking practice, go to page 148.

**A** **IN PAIRS** Read this statement and decide if you agree or disagree with it.

*The government should offer incentives to local businesses to support the local economy.*

**B** **IN GROUPS** Discuss how governments should support local businesses and how they can do it.

## LIFE SKILLS inquiry

**A** Read the definition of inquiry. In what ways can you investigate a topic?

Inquiry is the process of discovering more about a topic by asking questions or investigating it. Skillful inquiries include researching and interpreting information, asking questions, and then sharing and reflecting on the answers.

**B** You are going to read an article about cryptocurrencies. Label the questions (1–6) with the letters of the definitions (a–c) for the type of questions they are.

1 What is Bitcoin? _a_
2 When and by whom was Bitcoin started? _b_
3 How important is Bitcoin? _a_
4 How does blockchain technology work? _c_
5 What is the limit on the number of bitcoins? _c_
6 What are the future applications of blockchain technology? _b_

   **a** Gist questions—read the article quickly to understand the main ideas.
   **b** Scan questions—look for specific information in the article.
   **c** Detailed questions—read the article carefully for a deep understanding.

**C** 🔊 **1.04** Read the article and answer the questions from **B** in your notebook.

# Bitcoin and Blockchain Technology

In recent years, Bitcoin and other cryptocurrencies have become much more common. You can **convert** regular money into bitcoins online. You can then buy, sell, and **invest** bitcoins, and you can spend bitcoins at companies such as Microsoft. You can even use bitcoins to pay for a trip into space with Virgin Galactic! But what exactly is Bitcoin and how might the technology it is based on change our world in the future?

Most regular **currencies**, such as the US dollar, are controlled by a central bank. In the case of the dollar, the Federal Reserve controls the **supply** of money and generally makes sure there is enough money to meet **demand** but still maintain the value of the currency. The dollar is only worth something because the Federal Reserve supports the currency. However, Bitcoin is a digital currency without any central control. Its value is created by the blockchain technology behind it.

Bitcoin started in 2008 when an article describing a new digital currency was published under the name of Satoshi Nakamoto. Nakamoto is a mysterious person, and no one knows who he or she is. The following year, 2009, the first bitcoins appeared. Bitcoins are "mined" by computers solving very complicated mathematical problems in the Bitcoin system. For doing this, they are rewarded with bitcoins. Over time, these problems get harder to solve, and so it becomes harder to create bitcoins. This whole process will stop when there are 21 million bitcoins, and no more will be created. But don't think you can get rich easily by mining bitcoins. You need a warehouse full of specialized computers to do the kind of work the system requires.

So how do you spend bitcoins? It's all built around the blockchain. The blockchain is a record of every single transaction involving bitcoins since the currency started. Bitcoins are stored as encrypted strings of characters in digital wallets. When you send a bitcoin from your **account** to another account, computers on the network start to confirm that transaction. This is the mining work that earns bitcoins. When enough computers have confirmed it, it becomes part of the blockchain, and that bitcoin now belongs to the other person and is stored in their wallet.

Blockchain technology has applications in many other areas where we need to securely track things. For example, it could be used to locate and process all the parts involved in a business's supply chain, making manufacturing more efficient. This would lead to cheaper products. It could be used to create a secure digital voting system. And in a world of "the internet of things"—where devices, such as driverless cars, are connected and share data—blockchain technology can make communication between those devices safe and secure.

Bitcoin could be just the beginning of a data revolution.

---

### GLOSSARY

**cryptocurrency (n):** a digital currency that is independent of a central bank
**encrypted (adj):** in code
**mine (v):** earn bitcoins by doing calculations in the Bitcoin system

**D** **IN GROUPS** Share and compare your answers to the questions in **B**. Then discuss these questions.

1 How do the different types of questions help you find different types of information?
2 How does the process of asking questions help you understand a topic better?
3 What is the benefit of sharing and comparing your answers?
4 How do you think the process of inquiry will be important in your future career?

**MAKE IT DIGITAL**

Consider all you have learned about cryptocurrencies, and create a list of questions you still want to know the answers to. Research cryptocurrencies online, and produce a fact sheet.

## VOCABULARY finance vocabulary

**A** **Match each word from LIFE SKILLS C to the correct definition.**

1 Let me just see how much money I have in my savings **account**. _d_
2 Before we go on vacation, let's **convert** some dollars into euros. _f_
3 The **currency** of Canada is the Canadian dollar. _b_
4 The **demand** for automobiles that run on diesel is falling. _a_
5 Why don't you **invest** your money in shares in a large corporation? _c_
6 Home prices have increased because of a drop in the **supply** of new homes. _e_

**a** the amount of something that people want
**b** a system of money, often the one used in a particular country
**c** use your money to try to make a profit
**d** an arrangement where a bank, etc., looks after your money
**e** the amount of something that is available
**f** change something, such as money, into another form

## THINKING SKILL summarizing

**A** **Read about summarizing. In what situations is summarizing an important skill?**

We often need to summarize information. This is important when we need to communicate to another person what a long text, report, or book says. Good summarizing skills help save time and avoid misunderstanding. To summarize, we need to:

• identify the main ideas in a text.
• express the main ideas clearly. We do this using our own words rather than copying large parts of text from the original.
• check that our summary includes all the necessary information and does not include any unnecessary or irrelevant information.

**B** **IN PAIRS** Read this summary of the article in LIFE SKILLS C. Is it a good summary or a bad summary? Discuss how you might change it.

Bitcoin has become more popular. You can buy and sell bitcoins online, and you can spend bitcoins with companies such as Microsoft. You can even use bitcoins to pay for a trip into space with Virgin Galactic! Unlike the US dollar, Bitcoin isn't controlled by a central bank. It started around 2009. Computers mine bitcoins. You send bitcoins from your digital wallet to other people.

**C** **Write your own summary of the article in LIFE SKILLS C in your notebook.**

**D** **IN GROUPS** Discuss how summarizing can be helpful in your chosen career.

### 💬 MEDIATION CONFIDENT COMMUNICATOR working effectively in a group

**A   Read the dialogue. How does each person help the group to work effectively?**

**Logan:** So, we're going to give a presentation on future applications of blockchain technology. It's very complicated, so I think we need to plan how we're going to do it.

**Lia:** I agree. Should we brainstorm ideas together, or should we each spend a few minutes making notes of our ideas?

**Destiny:** I'm not sure. What do you think, Logan?

**Logan:** We could each choose an area and be responsible for that. So, I could research applications in business. And you, Lia, could look at applications in voting and ID. And maybe you could look at the internet of things, Destiny.

**Lia:** Sounds good. Before we start researching, should we just check that we all have the same understanding of what blockchain technology is?

**Destiny:** That's a good idea. Let's do that in a second. I think we also need to think about how we're going to present the information. Are we going to create an electronic presentation, and should we include images and video?

**Logan:** I'd say an electronic presentation with images to explain what we're talking about. We probably won't have enough time for video.

**Destiny:** OK, great. We're going to check our understanding together, then we're each going to research a separate area before we come together again to create an electronic presentation with images.

**Lia:** OK. We have a plan. So, let me explain what I think blockchain technology is, and you see if you agree!

**B   Read the instructions and answer the questions.**

In a group, you are going to give a presentation to the rest of the class. In your presentation, you should explain what you know about blockchain technology. You should also describe present and possible future applications of the technology.

1   What type of presentation (electronic, spoken, other) would you like to put together?
_____

2   What applications of blockchain technology would you like to focus on? _____
_____

3   What do you think is the best way of organizing the work? _____
_____

**C   IN GROUPS Discuss the task. Plan how you are going to work together to create your presentation. Make notes on what you decide in your notebook.**

**D   Give your presentation to the rest of the class.**

**E   Discuss the questions.**

1   In your discussion, did you ask questions to organize the work or suggest different ways of working? Do you feel your group worked together well?

2   Did anyone summarize the discussion at the end? Why do you think this is important?

## VOCABULARY review

SCORE: / 10

**A** Choose the correct words.

These days, it's relatively easy in most countries to start **1** out / up a company. You have an idea and identify the **2** demand / supply for a service or product. You register your company with the authorities, and you start trading. People do it without thinking about what an amazing thing the corporation or limited company is. This form of **3** business / trade enterprise is recognized as a separate legal entity, like a person. That means that it can conduct business, such as **4** exporting / importing goods to other countries, and the risk to each person who has **5** included / invested in the company is limited. Before this kind of company was developed in the 19th century, the possibility that you could personally lose everything when a company failed **6** put / set many people off getting involved in business. With the corporation or limited company, it became possible to **7** access / purchase shares in a company and know that you would not lose more money than the value of the shares that belong **8** to / with you, even if the company **9** closed / ended down. The idea took **10** off / up, and now it's possible to put your money into companies around the world.

## GRAMMAR review

SCORE: / 10

**A** Complete the sentences with the correct perfect form using the verb in parentheses.

**1** I was tired because I _____ (work) all morning.

**2** How long _____ (you/run) your own company?

**3** The manager _____ (leave) the office by the time I arrived, so I missed her.

**4** My parents' company _____ (export) products to Europe for the last 20 years.

**5** I _____ (set up) two very successful companies by the time I was 25.

 *Work book*

**B** Write *Correct* if the article in bold is correct and *Incorrect* if it is incorrect.

**1** The Danube is a river that has brought trade to many European cities. _correct_

**2** Do you think that **the** free trade is important for economic development? _incorrect_

**3** I applied for a job at **a** Museum of Modern Art in New York. _incorrect_

**4** Our company does a lot of business with **the** French. _incorrect_

**5** The currency in **the** Brazil is the real. _correct_

**16–20 correct:** You can use phrasal verbs and the language of trade and finance.
You can use articles and perfect forms of verbs.
**0–15 correct:** Look again at the Vocabulary and Grammar sections in the unit.

**TOTAL SCORE:** / 20

## EXAM SKILLS    SPEAKING have a two-way discussion

Look at the phrases below. In one minute, decide which are used for agreeing (*A*) or for disagreeing (*D*).

**1** I can see what you mean, but … _D_

**2** Yes, you have a good point. _A_

**3** I think … might be a better idea. _D_

**4** Totally. _A_

**5** I'm not so sure about that. _D_

**6** That's very true. _A_

Go to Exams Skills on page 128–129 to learn how to have a two-way discussion.

## WHAT DO YOU ALREADY KNOW?

**1 IN GROUPS** Think about the most popular sports in your country. Why are they popular? Are any of them dangerous?

## THINK AND PREPARE

**2** Decide whether you agree or disagree with this statement.

*Sports that are dangerous for people or animals should be banned.*

**3 IN GROUPS** Prepare to have a discussion about the statement. Make some notes about the points you want to make. Consider these points:

- cultural traditions and popular preferences
- economic opportunities or problems for athletes or communities
- possible solutions to specific dangers

**VIDEO**

Watch the video as you prepare to hold a discussion and find out how to persuade others.

## SPEAK YOUR MIND

**4** Discuss the topic. Try to persuade others to your point of view.

### In this unit, you will ...

- discuss ways to change sports and compare your group's opinions on sports.
- focus on Mediation: translate for informal communication.
- focus on a Thinking Skill: deducing.
- read about the use of biomechanics in sports.
- learn about equality: consider how different people receive different treatment.
- read about gathering diagnostic information and the professions that use this skill.

## READING

**A** **IN GROUPS** Discuss the questions.

1  What are your favorite sports?
2  What are the most exciting aspects of the sports you like?
3  Have your favorite sports or the athletes improved over time? If so, how have they improved?

**B** Scan the journal article. See how many of the ways to improve sports you mentioned are in the text.

# Applications and Issues in Biomechanics

**by Bruce Martin**

1  The field of biomechanics is increasingly important in the modern world. Biomechanics is the science of movement of humans and animals. It combines ideas from physics, engineering, and biology in order to understand how internal and external forces interact during different types of movement. Biomechanics is important in fields as varied as office furniture design, physical therapy, medical equipment design, and perhaps most extensively, sports and exercise science.

2  In sports, biomechanics has many different applications. First, it is used to study athletes' movement in order to help them improve their performance. For example, an American football coach **records** the players as they pass the ball in order to analyze the position and movement of the passers' heads, arms, or feet. This allows coaches to observe players passing the ball from many different angles and to recognize problems that can be corrected to make their passing more effective.

3  Sports equipment manufacturers spend years trying to come up with new types of shoes, clothing, and equipment that will improve athletic performance, and biomechanics helps designers know what types of improvements will be most useful. In today's high-tech world, athletes have an easier time getting to the top in their sports if they have the latest, best equipment. We see athletes of all types breaking more and more **records** in part because of technical innovations in their clothing and equipment.

4  Finally, one of the most important applications of biomechanics is in the area of sports injuries, both in prevention and treatment. Research in the field of biomechanics helps coaches and sports doctors understand the types of movements and impacts that cause injuries. By studying how muscles, tendons, and ligaments move and exert force, medical professionals can decrease the frequency of injuries. Furthermore, biomechanics plays a big role when injuries do occur. Using modern physical therapy techniques and equipment often means that athletes have less difficulty recovering from injuries than in the past.

5  Biomechanics has helped sports and athletes in many ways. Nevertheless, there is a disadvantage to the advances in biomechanics. While movement studies **produce** better equipment and some safer practices in sports, they also increase athletic ability in ways that make certain sports more dangerous. One example is American football. Players are bigger and stronger than they used to be, and they understand how to use their bodies for maximum efficiency. Some say this has led to an **increase** in injuries in this sport.

6  Constant advances in biomechanics and other sciences make sports more exciting for fans. If sports are exciting, then more fans watch. Advertisers pay to advertise during televised sports events, and fans pay to attend or watch those events, so everyone is happy. We can't **discount** the importance of fans' enthusiasm, but should there be limits to improving performance? Should a better understanding of the physics of injuries lead to a ban on tackling in American football or heading in soccer? It is difficult for many fans to imagine sitting around watching football or soccer without those things, but is it ethical to allow players to continue to do things that may permanently damage their health?

---

**GLOSSARY**

**ethical (adj):** in a way that is right
**exert (v):** to use influence or force to make something happen
**innovation (n):** a new idea, product, or way of doing something

**C** 🔊 **2.01 Read the article again and complete the notes.**

1  A definition of biomechanics: _is the science of Moviment of human & animals._
2  Sciences included in biomechanics: _physics, engineering & biology_
3  General uses of biomechanics: _office furniture design, physical therapy & sports_
4  Applications of biomechanics in sports: _Improve their performance, equipments & sports,_
5  A negative effect of increasing athletic ability: _increase athletic ability, in ways that may injuries_
6  The result of scientific advances for sports fans: _Sports more exiting more fans._

_Artun Sports more dangerous._

**D** **IN PAIRS READING SKILL—Identify opinions** Look back at the journal article and discuss the questions.

1  In paragraph 5, how does the writer indicate that he is not the only one who thinks that greater efficiency in athletes causes more injuries? _Some says this ..._
2  Does the writer think biomechanics has had only positive effects on sports? What example does he use to support his opinion? _NO / Never theless._
3  What is the purpose of the questions in the last paragraph? _this about others ways_

## VOCABULARY  nouns and verbs with the same form

**A** Complete the sentences using the words in bold in READING **B**. Write *N* (noun) or *V* (verb) after each sentence.

1  Scientists in biomechanics can't _discount_ the feedback from athletes if they want the best results. ✓
2  I'm doing _research_ on biomechanics for my biology class. _N_
3  Biomechanics helps workers who use repetitive movements, e.g., workers picking lettuce, tomatoes, and other types of _produce_ _N_.
4  With his new fitness app, my friend _records_ his daily workouts to check his progress. ✓
5  Some of the new fitness monitors are so expensive that there has been a _decrease_ in sales. _N_
6  As fitness monitors _they are produce_ the amount of data we have on physical movement, biomechanics will become more specialized. ✓

⭐ **MAKE IT YOURS**

Think about people you know who monitor their fitness. What do they record? What other health and fitness words would you like to know in English?

## PRONUNCIATION  nouns and verbs with the same form

**A** 🔊 **2.02 Listen and underline the stressed syllable in each word. Then practice saying the words.**

| Noun | record | increase | decrease | produce | discount | research |
|------|--------|----------|----------|---------|----------|----------|
| Verb | record | increase | decrease | produce | discount | research |

**B** **IN PAIRS** Look back at the sentences in VOCABULARY **A**. Make a sentence with the form of each word that was not used in the exercise.

## GRAMMAR verb + gerund

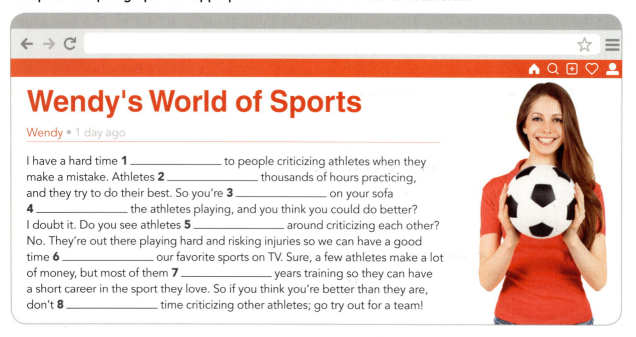

**A** Look back at the underlined sentences and phrases in READING **B** and add words to the table.

| | |
|---|---|
| **1** *have* + object + gerund<br>*We had fun playing tennis.* | objects: *fun, trouble, a good/easy/hard time,*<br>_____ |
| **2** verb of perception + object + gerund<br>*We heard her giving a presentation.* | verbs: *notice, hear, listen, watch,* _____,<br>_____ |
| **3** *spend/waste* + time expression + gerund<br>*I waste time surfing the internet.* | time: *time, a long time, your life,* _____ |
| **4** *sit/stand/lie* + expression of place + gerund<br>*Don't just sit there doing nothing.* | place: *there, on the sofa/bed, at your desk,*<br>_____ |

For more practice, go to page 158.

**B** Complete the paragraph with appropriate verbs from **A** in the correct form.

# Wendy's World of Sports

Wendy • 1 day ago

I have a hard time **1** _____ to people criticizing athletes when they make a mistake. Athletes **2** _____ thousands of hours practicing, and they try to do their best. So you're **3** _____ on your sofa **4** _____ the athletes playing, and you think you could do better? I doubt it. Do you see athletes **5** _____ around criticizing each other? No. They're out there playing hard and risking injuries so we can have a good time **6** _____ our favorite sports on TV. Sure, a few athletes make a lot of money, but most of them **7** _____ years training so they can have a short career in the sport they love. So if you think you're better than they are, don't **8** _____ time criticizing other athletes; go try out for a team!

**C** **IN PAIRS** Discuss the questions.

**1** What do you spend most of your time each day doing? Is there anything you frequently waste time doing?

**2** Are you very active on weekends, or do you often lie around watching TV or doing nothing?

**3** Do you have fun watching sports, or do you prefer to play a sport? If you play a sport, what do you have the most difficulty doing?

**4** When you see people or animals getting injured in a sport, does it change your opinion of the sport?

## SPEAKING

For more speaking practice, go to page 148.

**A** Read the statements and decide which ones you agree or disagree with.

**1** There should be no limits to technology that improves athletes' performance.

**2** Children should not be allowed to play games that are physically dangerous like soccer and football.

**3** Heading in soccer and tackling in football should be banned.

**B** **IN GROUPS** Share your opinions and see who agrees or disagrees with you.

## VOCABULARY business and economics

**A Match the words to the definitions.**

> allocate   corporate sponsor   individual donor   investment   fund   funding   socioeconomic   sponsorship

1 _____: to officially give something, often money, for a specific purpose
2 _____: related to social and economic level in a society
3 _____: to provide money for something that costs a lot
4 _____: a company that gives money to support an activity or program
5 _____: money that a person receives in support from a company
6 _____: money from an organization for a specific purpose
7 _____: a private citizen who gives money to support a cause
8 _____: an amount of money put into a project to make profit or get an advantage

**B Complete the paragraph with the correct forms of the words from A.**

My city has a program that teaches young children to play sports. The government
1 _____ part of the program, and the rest of the 2 _____
comes from 3 _____ and 4 _____. Part of the money is
5 _____ to salaries for coaches, and the rest is spent on equipment and facilities. It's
a great program because it gives kids from lower 6 _____ levels an opportunity to
learn and practice a sport. The best kids even get 7 _____ from famous companies.
The government sees this as an 8 _____ because it gives the kids a positive future.

## LIFE SKILLS equality

**A Read the definition of equality. Which other areas in life can reflect inequality?**

Equality is the right of all the various groups in society to be treated the same way. People working to make society equal often look for areas in life where there are differences and try to reduce those differences. This can include work, leisure activities, entertainment, etc.

**B IN PAIRS Discuss the questions in reference to sports in your country.**

1 How do you think training for major sports events like the Olympics or the World Cup is funded? Do all sports teams receive an equal amount of funding? If not, who receives more?
2 What other inequalities in sports do you think exist in your country?
3 In your opinion, which inequalities are the most important ones to solve?

**C 2.03 Listen to a discussion on inequality in sports among students majoring in sports management. Complete the notes. Listen again to check your answers.**

How sports programs and athletes are funded:
1 In the USA: _____ or _____
2 In other countries: usually _____

Issues of inequality in sports:
3 _____
4 _____
5 _____

**D IN GROUPS Discuss these questions on equality.**

1 How can discussing issues of equality in sports help you understand general issues of equality?
2 What issues of equality are there in your profession?

 **MAKE IT DIGITAL**

Research different sports online, and find out which ones have the fewest areas of inequality and which have the most. Create a list of recommendations for young people hoping to play those sports.

## GRAMMAR relative pronouns with –*ever* and *no matter*

**A** Study the examples in the table, then choose the correct option.

**1** Pronouns with –*ever* are used to talk about …

    **a** a specific time, place, thing, or person.

    **b** a general time, place, thing, or person.

**2** *No matter* + a pronoun means …

    **a** something is true in all cases.

    **b** there is a problem with the situation.

| | |
|---|---|
| pronoun + verb | **Whoever says** that anyone can have a sports career doesn't understand how the system in this country works. |
| pronoun + subject + verb | I think **wherever you go**, you'll find inequality in sports opportunities. |
| pronoun + object + subject + verb | **Whatever sports the media covers the most** are the ones people are going to be most interested in.<br><br>**Whichever issue we choose**, we need to present all sides of it so the class can discuss it. |
| *no matter* + pronoun + clause | So I guess **no matter what country you're from**, inequality in sports is a problem. |

For more practice, go to page 159.

**B** Complete the sentences with the words from the box.

however   no matter   whatever   whenever   wherever   whoever

**1** _____ sport is on TV at the moment, I watch it.

**2** _____ the Olympics are held, even in a different time zone, I watch them live.

**3** _____ my country is playing a game in the World Cup, I watch the game, even if I have to take off from work or school.

**4** _____ what soccer teams are playing, I watch the games. I love soccer!

**5** I don't mind who wins or loses. I enjoy the game, _____ it turns out.

**6** _____ says soccer is boring doesn't understand the game.

**C** **IN PAIRS** Discuss whether you agree or disagree with the statements in B. Explain why.

## WRITING a survey

**A** **IN PAIRS** Look at a survey on using tax money for sports in Canada and identify the most popular uses.

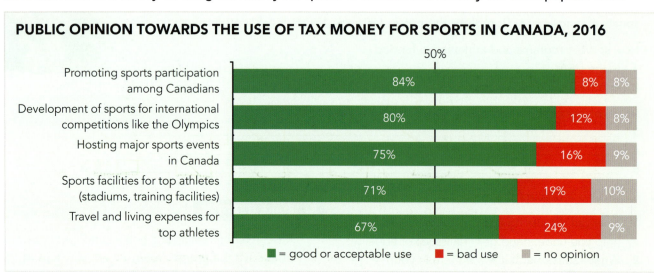

**PUBLIC OPINION TOWARDS THE USE OF TAX MONEY FOR SPORTS IN CANADA, 2016**

- Promoting sports participation among Canadians: 84% / 8% / 8%
- Development of sports for international competitions like the Olympics: 80% / 12% / 8%
- Hosting major sports events in Canada: 75% / 16% / 9%
- Sports facilities for top athletes (stadiums, training facilities): 71% / 19% / 10%
- Travel and living expenses for top athletes: 67% / 24% / 9%

■ = good or acceptable use   ■ = bad use   ■ = no opinion

**B** Complete the summary of the survey using the phrases from the box.

> 80% support   majority   slightly fewer   strong support   three-fourths of

**Survey Summary**

In 2016, a Canadian organization surveyed Canadians on the use of tax money to fund sports. The survey showed the following:

- The **1** _____ of participants in the survey say that using money to encourage Canadians to participate in sports is good or acceptable, while **2** _____ government funding of sports for international competitions.
- The use of tax money to host major international sports events is supported by **3** _____ Canadians.
- There is also **4** _____ for funding sports facilities for top athletes (71%).
- While it is true that **5** _____ Canadians support paying living and travel expenses for high-performance athletes (67%), there is still a majority of support for it.

In conclusion, the majority of Canadians support the use of tax money for sports, both among Canadians and for high-level international sports competitions and athletes.

**C** Talk to five classmates. Find out whether they support each type of funding in the table.

| Type of Funding | 1 | 2 | 3 | 4 | 5 |
|---|---|---|---|---|---|
| Promoting public sports participation | | | | | |
| Development of sports for international competitions | | | | | |
| Hosting international events | | | | | |
| Sports facilities for top athletes | | | | | |
| Travel and living expenses for top athletes | | | | | |

Key: Good use of government funds: ✓, Bad use of government funds: X, No opinion: ?

**D** Use your survey to write a summary of how people in your class feel about government funding for sports. Try to use phrases from the summary.

## SPEAKING

For more speaking practice, go to page 148.

**A** Read the statements. Then, write the numbers (1–4) on the line below to show how much you agree with each one.

**1** On TV, we see only the most popular and commercial sports. The networks should be forced to cover less well-known sports, too, to give them an opportunity to become more popular.

**2** Whoever wants to learn a sport should have the opportunity, no matter what their socioeconomic level is. Public tax money should be used to promote and support sports training for children and teens.

**3** All schools should have to include sports training in their budgets so that kids can start learning sports at an early age.

**4** The government should allocate equal funding to all the Olympic sports that our country participates in, no matter how popular the sport is.

| Strongly Agree | Agree | Neutral | Disagree | Strongly Disagree |
|---|---|---|---|---|

**B** **IN GROUPS** Compare your answers. Find out whether the majority of the group agrees or disagrees with each statement.

# LISTENING

**A** **IN PAIRS** Look at the photos of sports and decide which are currently included in the Olympics. Which of these sports do people in your country participate in?

curling

shooting

rhythmic gymnastics

bowling

synchronized swimming

sport climbing

squash

rollerblading

**B** 🔊 **2.04** Listen to a conversation about the Olympics and check which sports are included in the Olympics.

**C** 🔊 **2.04 LISTENING SKILL—Understand attitude** Listen again. Choose the speakers' attitudes toward different Olympic sports. Then choose how you were able to decide the answer.

**1** Carly **thinks** / **doesn't think** it's unfair to include basketball in the Olympics.
   **a** tone of voice          **b** words used          **c** both

**2** Carly **is** / **isn't** convinced by Andrew's argument about basketball.
   **a** tone of voice          **b** words used          **c** both

**3** Carly **thinks** / **doesn't think** zorbing would be a good Olympic sport.
   **a** tone of voice          **b** words used          **c** both

**4** Andrew **thinks** / **doesn't think** adding dancing to the Olympics is a bad idea.
   **a** tone of voice          **b** words used          **c** both

**5** Carly **agrees** / **doesn't agree** that break dancing is similar to gymnastics.
   **a** tone of voice          **b** words used          **c** both

> 💡 **MAKE IT REAL**
>
> Common ways to express disagreement are *You gotta be kidding! Seriously? That's so not true. That's lame.*

# VOCABULARY adjective and adverb collocations

**A** **IN PAIRS** Discuss the questions.

**1** Which sports do you think are the most **physically demanding**?
**2** Which do you think are more **mentally challenging**: individual sports or team sports?
**3** Which Olympic sports do you think are the most **internationally popular**?
**4** Which Olympic sports are not **widely played** in your country?
**5** **Broadly speaking**, do you think the Summer or Winter Olympics are more exciting? Why?
**6** Is it **generally accepted** that your national government should fund Olympic athletes?

**B** **IN PAIRS** Use the words in **A** in different combinations to make sentences about sports.

*I think it is broadly accepted that soccer is the most internationally popular sport.*

# THINKING SKILL  deducing

**A  IN PAIRS** Read about deductive reasoning. Then deduce which of the two hypotheses below is true.

Deductive reasoning starts with a hypothesis and then examines the supporting statements to reach a conclusion about whether the hypothesis is true or not. For example, for the hypothesis "Snow is cold," you could have two statements: Statement one: All frozen water is cold. Statement two: Snow is a type of frozen water. Looking at the supporting statements, it is logical to deduce that it is true that snow is cold.

Hypothesis 1: Fred is in excellent physical condition.

Statement 1: Fred is an Olympic swimmer.

Statement 2: All Olympic swimmers are in excellent physical condition.

Is the hypothesis true? _____

Hypothesis 2: Joe is an Olympic swimmer.

Statement 1: Joe is a swimmer.

Statement 2: Joe is in excellent physical condition.

Is the hypothesis true? _____

**B  IN GROUPS** Use the statements describing the sports that should be included in the Olympics to make deductions about the hypothesis below. Discuss each sport in relation to the statements.

Hypothesis: All of the sports in the pictures in **LISTENING A** should stay in the Olympics or be added to the Olympics.

Statements: To be included in the Olympics, a sport must fulfil a majority of these criteria:

- have a history of being included in the Olympics
- be broadly popular with the public
- be interesting to many different ages of people
- be widely played in a variety of countries
- have the possibility of gender equality (events for both men and women)
- be physically demanding

**C  Discuss the questions as a class.**

1  How difficult was it for your group to agree on whether or not a sport should be included in the Olympics?
2  Did you consider some of the statements to be more important than others? If so, which ones?

**MEDIATION CONFIDENT COMMUNICATOR** translating for informal communication

**A** **Discuss the questions as a class.**

**1** Have you ever seen someone acting as an informal translator to help people communicate in English and your language? What was the situation?

**2** What do you imagine someone needs to consider when they are translating informally?

**B** **Complete the tips for translating in an informal situation using the phrases from the box.**

> ask for clarification   do not give your own opinions   do not interrupt   enough information   one at a time

**1** When you are translating during a group conversation, ask people to speak _____ to give you a chance to translate what each person says.

**2** You don't have to translate every word, but make sure you give _____ to provide an accurate translation.

**3** If the conversation includes opinions, _____ while translating what someone else has said. Try to translate the opinions as accurately as possible.

**4** If you are not sure about what someone has said, _____ before trying to translate the idea to another person.

**5** If someone is translating for you, _____ while the person is listening to others speak. You can ask questions when they have finished speaking.

**C** **IN GROUPS Read the instructions. Then discuss the questions below.**

You are having a discussion with a group of friends. There is an English-speaking visitor, so you are speaking English because the visitor doesn't speak your language. The problem is that one of your friends speaks very little English, so you will need to say everything in both English and your own language so everyone can participate in the conversation. Decide who will be the English-speaking visitor and who will be the non-English speaker. The other people in the group should take turns translating for those two people during the discussion.

**1** Look at the list of Olympic sports. Should any of these sports not be included in the Olympics? If not, why not?

- curling
- golf
- rhythmic gymnastics
- rugby
- shooting
- skateboarding
- sport climbing
- synchronized swimming
- surfing
- table tennis

**2** What sports or games that are not currently in the Olympics do you think should be included?

*A: I think curling is a weird sport, and anyway, only a few countries do it.*

*B: I'm sorry, I don't understand.*

*C: I'll translate. He said …*

**D** **Discuss the questions as a class.**

**1** Did it work well for more than one person to translate, or would it have worked better to have just one translator?

**2** Broadly speaking, was everyone able to communicate their ideas and participate equally in the conversation? If not, how could you make the translation process work better in future situations?

## VOCABULARY review

SCORE: / 10

**A** Complete the text entry with the words and phrases from the box.

| | | | | |
|---|---|---|---|---|
| allocate | broadly speaking | corporate sponsors | decrease | funding |
| generally accepted | increase | physically demanding | research | widely played |

I believe that the government should **1** _____ more money for **2** _____ on
**3** _____ sports like football. It is especially important for scientists to have
**4** _____ for studies on how these sports affect child athletes. Football and soccer are very
popular in schools and are **5** _____ by even very young children. Modern technology has
caused an **6** _____ in injuries in these sports, and this is very dangerous to all players, but
especially children. It is **7** _____ that there is a certain level of risk in any sport, but shouldn't
we do everything we can to make sports safe? Some research programs have **8** _____,
but we need independent studies that are not done by companies who want to sell their products.
**9** _____, I am in favor of children playing sports, but I just think the government should
provide for studies to help **10** _____ sports injuries.

## GRAMMAR review

SCORE: / 10

**A** Complete the sentences with the words and phrases from the box.

| | | | | |
|---|---|---|---|---|
| a hard time | a lot of fun | heard | sitting around | spend a lot of time |

**1** Sometimes I have _____ understanding the rules of certain sports.
**2** I love being active. I hate _____ doing nothing.
**3** My friends and I _____ watching sports on weekends.
**4** I _____ some people talking about how dangerous sports are, but I don't agree.
**5** You can have _____ doing exercise if you do it by playing a sport.

**B** Complete the paragraph with *no matter* and pronouns with *–ever*.

**1** _____ you go in the world, you see people watching and playing soccer. I guess it's
the most widely played sport in the world, and **2** _____ says it's boring hasn't seen a
dramatic World Cup final! **3** _____ someone complains that the players don't score
enough, I remind them that there are lots of games with low scores, such as American football. Of course,
if you don't understand the game, you won't like it. That's true for **4** _____ sport you
watch, but some people I know don't think soccer is exciting, **5** _____ what I say.

**16–20 correct:** You can use adjectives, adverbs, verbs, nouns, and the language of
business and economics.
You can use verbs with gerunds, and relative pronouns.
**0–15 correct:** Look again at the Vocabulary and Grammar sections in the unit.

TOTAL SCORE: / 20

## SKILLS FOR PROS
Diagnostic Information Gathering

Read this quote. What do you think it means?

**"The man who asks a question is
a fool for a minute, the man who
does not ask is a fool for life."**

—Confucius

Turn to Skills for Pros on page 130.

# Medicine on the Mend

## WHAT DO YOU ALREADY KNOW?

**1  IN GROUPS** Think about the common medical issues that exist in your country and any medical advances that have been developed to deal with those issues. Discuss these questions.
- What medical issues were a problem in the past but are not a problem now?
- Are there still medical issues that modern medicine is unable to deal with?
- How do people in your community get access to information to help with any medical issues they have?

## THINK AND PREPARE

**2**  Decide whether you agree or disagree with this statement.

*Doctors will never know how to cure all medical issues.*

**3  IN PAIRS** Prepare a role-play between two members of your community: an older person and a younger person. The older person has more traditional beliefs about how to stay healthy. The younger person is aware of modern medicine and how it has developed. Make notes about your position and reasons. Consider these points:
- trust in technology versus trust in traditions
- the extent to which modern medicine can deal with medical issues
- how people today get access to information about traditional and modern medicine

 **VIDEO**
Watch the video as you prepare to do a role-play and find out how to use body language effectively.

## SPEAK YOUR MIND

**4**  Perform your role-play for the class.

### In this unit, you will ...

- discuss medical services and present a health-related tech product.
- focus on Mediation: develop intercultural communication.
- focus on Thinking Skills: analyzing.
- read about medical services across the globe.
- learn about critical literacy: look at different types of medical information.
- practice your general exam skills by scanning questions to decide which ones to answer first.

## READING

**A** **IN PAIRS READING SKILL—Predict content using visuals** Look at the photos. Brainstorm as many words as you can for each one. Compare your list with a partner. Based on your lists, what do you think the text will be about?

a paramedic

a medical doctor

a medical advice website

a pharmacist

**B** 🔊 **3.01** Read the article. Then choose *True* or *False* for the statements that follow.

# Medical Services: Changing Lives Across the Globe

With tens of millions of the world's people experiencing difficulties with accessing health services, businesses are interested in bringing health care solutions to the global market. Journalist Luiz Sousa went to investigate.

Busara Chande sits on the steps outside her hut in rural Tanzania, **recovering from** the birth of twins. "I'm so happy they're here," she says, holding back tears. "Niku almost didn't make it. If the taxi ambulance service didn't exist, I'm sure he wouldn't have survived. As it is, he is just perfect." Busara's story is unusual because both her babies survived, due largely to a service based entirely on cell phones. When Busara realized her babies were on the way, she used her cell phone to call a health worker who connected her to one of the 130 taxi drivers operating in the charity network. The nearest driver to Busara, Noel Abasi, **responded to** the call. Without such a service, Busara would probably have had to walk to the hospital or if she were very lucky, she would have gone by ambulance. Unfortunately, her region has only two ambulances for a population of 500,000. Noel's taxi, which cost a mere $40 for the charity (a large amount for Busara), potentially saved the lives of three people.

A thousand miles from Tanzania, in Rwanda, another medical service is being tested, with amazing results. It is the world's first national delivery service for medication and blood for blood transfusions, which only uses drones. The battery-operated drones provide a lifesaving service delivering blood to 13 million people. Sometimes the deliveries are made to hospitals or clinics and sometimes to individuals in hard-to-reach areas. One person who benefited from these deliveries is a farmer, Sebahive, who **suffers from** a respiratory disease. If he had lived in the capital city, medication would be available for him at his local clinic. But 28 minutes after calling the emergency drone service, the medication had been delivered. "I have five children. If the drone hadn't arrived, they would be orphans now," says Sebahive.

On the other side of the world is a medical camp where refugees are **provided with** access to essential medical services they have been **deprived of**. Tariq is from Iran and was **affected by** severe stomach pain, but with no English, he was unable to explain his symptoms. Fortunately, he was able to use a new app for translators. This new app recommends one of over 8,000 volunteer translators based on the language they speak and the area of medicine they **specialize in**. The translator can then offer advice about what to do. "Luckily," says Tariq's wife, "the volunteer **translated into** Farsi for us, and they were able to diagnose appendicitis and transfer him to a hospital."

What is clear is that these innovative business ideas have made a real difference to groups of people across the globe—simple but practical solutions that really can, and do, save lives.

### GLOSSARY

**blood transfusions** (n): taking blood from one person and giving it to another in a medical emergency

1 Busara used a GPS to find the nearest taxi ambulance to her.          True / False
2 Busara paid $40 for the taxi ambulance service.          True / False
3 The drones are able access remote areas.          True / False
4 Tariq communicated with the volunteer in his native language.          True / False

**C** **IN GROUPS** Discuss the questions.

1  Is health care free in your country?
2  Do you think universal free health care for everyone will ever become a reality?

## VOCABULARY dependent prepositions

**A** Match the words in bold from READING B to make sentences.

1  Could you translate these medical records _____
2  Every spring, Jack suffers _____
3  My medical school specializes _____
4  Layton's health has been badly affected _____
5  Children should not be deprived _____
6  Are hospital patients provided _____
7  The nurse immediately responded _____
8  It took Jim a long time to recover _____

a  of an education, no matter what their circumstances are.
b  in pediatric medicine.
c  with a choice of foods for meals?
d  into Spanish for me, please?
e  to the man's cry for help.
f  from the injuries he got in the accident.
g  by his poor diet and lack of exercise.
h  from allergies because of all the flowers.

**B** Write a verb and dependent preposition from **A** next to its definition.

1  _____: to get better; improve (for health)
2  _____: to have an illness, disease, or medical condition
3  _____: to change one language into another
4  _____: to react to a situation by doing what is needed
5  _____: to be changed or influenced by something, usually negatively
6  _____: to not have enough of something that is essential
7  _____: to study a particular subject
8  _____: to give someone something they want or need

⭐ **MAKE IT YOURS**

Did you or someone you know have any illnesses as a child?
Go online to find the words in English to describe the illnesses.

## GRAMMAR mixed conditionals

**A** Read the sentences from READING B and write the correct tense to complete the grammar rules.

Verbs in green are unreal actions in the present.
Verbs in red are unreal actions in the past.

| | |
|---|---|
| "If the taxi ambulance service didn't exist, I'm sure he wouldn't have survived." | (But the taxi ambulance service does exist, so he did survive.) |
| "If the drone hadn't arrived, they would be orphans now," says Sebahive. | (But the drone did arrive, so they aren't orphans now.) |

Mixed conditional describing the unreal present result of an unreal past condition

If he had lived in the capital city, medication would be available …

| | |
|---|---|
| If + 1 _____ (If this thing had happened) | 2 _____ conditional (that thing would happen) |

Mixed conditional describing the unreal past result of an unreal present or continuing condition

If she were very lucky, she would have gone by ambulance.

| | |
|---|---|
| If + 3 _____ (If this thing happened) | 4 _____ conditional (that thing would have happened) |

For more practice, go to page 160.

**B** Complete the mixed conditional sentences with the correct form of the verbs in parentheses.

1 If Anna _____ (pass) her medical exams, she _____ (be) a doctor now.

2 I _____ (buy) the polka-dot T-shirt if I _____ (be) you.

3 I _____ (go) to the party last night if I _____ (not have) so much work to do.

4 If Vic _____ (not busy), he _____ (take) you to your doctor's appointment.

5 Greg _____ (invite) you for lunch yesterday if he _____ (know) about your trip!

**C** **IN PAIRS** Complete these sentences for you and then share your ideas with a partner.

1 If I had studied another language in high school, I would probably be _____ .

2 I wouldn't be _____ if I had been born in a different country.

3 If I didn't have to study, I would have _____ .

4 I would have _____ if I were rich.

# SPEAKING

For more speaking practice, go to page 149.

**A** **IN PAIRS** Look at the front page of the newspaper and discuss what you think the story is about.

## THE DAILY NEWS

www.thedailynews.com          THE WORLD'S FAVORITE NEWSPAPER          – since 1975

## INJURY INSPIRES INNOVATION

Many of us will remember star soccer player Jim Jackson: the youngest ever player to be picked for the Eagles in 2015. A severe injury after a horrible tackle in his first season meant the end of his soccer career at the age of 19. But while his career was affected by the injury, it was also the reason he was inspired to offer his services in creating the DMX—a leg cast that creates the perfect conditions to help athletes recover from injuries before they even reach the hospital. This invention has made Jim Jackson a millionaire, and more importantly, it has helped thousands of athletes in dozens of different sports.

**B** Think of all the different present results of Jim Jackson's injury.

*A: If he hadn't been injured, he would be a soccer player now.*

*B: True. But also if he hadn't been injured, the DMX wouldn't exist.*

**C** **IN GROUPS** Compare your ideas and see who thought of the largest number of results.

**D** **IN GROUPS** Discuss the questions.

1 What examples can you think of where a positive result came out of a negative situation?

2 What can you learn from the Jim Jackson story?

## LISTENING

**A** **IN PAIRS** You are going to listen to a radio show about technological innovations in medicine such as the one in the photograph. Before you listen, discuss what technological innovations you are aware of and what impact they might have.

**B** 🔊 **3.02** Now listen to check which of the innovations you thought of are mentioned. Make notes on the innovations that are mentioned and discuss with your partner which inventions you think are the most useful.

> **GLOSSARY**
>
> dementia (n): a serious illness, usually of old age, that affects the brain and the memory

**C** 🔊 **3.03 LISTENING SKILL—Use context clues to infer meaning** One way to understand unknown vocabulary is to try and understand the meaning of the word by hearing it in context. Listen to these sentences. Can you understand the meaning of the words that you don't know? Write your ideas.

1 advancements (noun plural) possible meaning: _____
2 biotechnology (noun) possible meaning: _____
3 pharmaceuticals (noun plural) possible meaning: _____
4 life expectancy (noun) possible meaning: _____
5 clone (verb) possible meaning: _____
6 practitioners (noun plural) possible meaning: _____

**D** **IN PAIRS** Compare your ideas. Listen again and check.

**E** **IN PAIRS** Talk about which innovation from the radio show you think is the most interesting and give reasons.

## VOCABULARY medical terms

**A** Write a word from the box next to its definition.

> antibiotics  eliminate  infection  limbs  organs  transplant  vaccinate  wounds

1 _____: arms or legs
2 _____: to be treated with a medicine to protect you from a disease
3 _____: to get rid of something, especially something bad
4 _____: parts of your body that do a specific job
5 _____: medications that cure an illness that is caused by bacteria
6 _____: medical operation where a person's organ is put into the body of someone else
7 _____: injuries where the skin is damaged, usually seriously
8 _____: a disease that is caused by bacteria or a virus

> 💡 **MAKE IT REAL**
>
> Instead of saying *getting vaccinated*, people normally say *getting shots*, e.g., *I was told I needed to get shots to travel to South America.*

## PRONUNCIATION silent letters

**A** Look at the words. Underline the silent consonant in each word.

1 pneumonia        2 limb        3 science        4 honor        5 designed

**B** 🔊 3.04 IN PAIRS Listen and check. Practice saying the words in pairs.

## GRAMMAR clauses of contrast and purpose

**A** Complete the grammar rules with a word or phrase from the box.

> base form    clause    gerund (x2)    modal verb    noun phrase    subject
>
> Clauses of purpose are used to express the use or purpose of a thing or to express why someone does or uses something:
> 1   These pills are for **getting** rid of headaches. *for +* _____
> 2   I used a bandage in order to **stop** the bleeding. *so as (not) to / in order (not) to +* _____
> 3   He's studying medicine so that **he can** become a doctor. *so (that) + subject +* _____ *+ clause*
>
> Clauses of contrast are used when you want to compare two things or two situations:
> 4   Despite **feeling** sick, Lucie went to work. *Despite / In spite of +* _____
> 5   In spite of **her cold**, Gaby went to the party. *Despite / In spite of +* _____
> 6   Despite the fact that **he failed his exams**, Kieran went on to become a pharmacist. *Despite / In spite of the fact that +* _____
> 7   Even though **she** was busy, the nurse managed to treat all her patients. *Even though / Although +* _____ *+ verb*
>
> For more practice, go to page 161.

**B** Complete the sentences from LISTENING **B** with a clause of contrast and purpose from the box.

> despite    even though    for    so as to    so that

1   One such device measures about 2 mm. by 2 mm. and, _____ it's tiny, it promises to help physicians check a patient's eating habits …
2   The developers claim that the responsive sensors on the device can be adapted _____ it can be worn on the skin …
3   For example, some medicines can now be adapted to the individual patient _____ treat whatever condition they have.
4   _____ it being in the early stages of development, Israeli scientists at Tel Aviv University have already created a small heart from human tissue.
5   Medical teams will be able to reproduce fully functioning organs _____ operating on transplant patients.

**C** Read the sentences in **B** again and answer the questions.

1   In which sentence could you also use *in order to*? _____
2   In which sentence could you also use *in spite of*? _____
3   In which sentence could you also use *although*? _____

**D** IN PAIRS Complete these sentences with your own ideas. Share your ideas with a partner.

1   Even though antibiotics are useful in some cases …
2   Although transplant surgery is risky …
3   In order to stay fit and healthy, people should …

## WRITING a blog post

**A** Look at the photo in the blog post. What do you think this device is used for?

**B** Read the blog post. Were you correct?

### Medical Tech—Looking to the Future

posted by AdrianTechGuru 02/27/20 at 13:32

I wanted to take this opportunity to share with you a medical tech innovation that I think is truly amazing. The eSight 3 looks like a headset that fits over your eyes—much like a virtual reality headset, although smaller and lighter. Instead of trying to make a digital world look more realistic, it uses a high-speed HD camera to create a video image and allows users with sight problems the ability to see things around them in a much clearer way.

The device is fully portable, which means wearers can use it in most situations, and the battery lasts up to six hours. The challenges of designing such a device were that wearers needed to be able to see their surroundings in real time and have maximum vision so as not to feel dizzy or lose their balance. It is designed to focus automatically, allows users to zoom between near and far objects, and can also capture screen shots or record images in the same way as a smartphone camera.

The device costs about $5,950, but the founders offer assistance and advice for people on the best way to raise funds. In spite of high production costs, they hope the price will fall over time and that similar, cheaper devices will become available to everyone who needs one.

Feel free to tell me about any other innovative medical tech products that you've come across.

**C** You are going to write a response to Adrian. Before you start, read this step-by-step guide to writing a blog post.

**Step 1:** Plan your blog post by choosing a topic, creating an outline, and checking facts. Make sure you choose a topic that interests you, as this will help with the writing.

**Step 2:** Decide on a headline that is informative and will capture your reader's attention.

**Step 3:** Write your blog post. Try not to write more than about 200 words.

**Step 4:** Edit your post. Read your post aloud to check that it flows. Don't be afraid to cut text or adapt your writing at the last minute.

**D** Write your blog post. Try to include clauses of contrast and purpose from GRAMMAR A.

**E** **IN GROUPS** Share your ideas. Which innovative product do you think is best and why?

## SPEAKING

For more speaking practice, go to page 149.

**A** Imagine that you have seen this competition online. Read the instructions and think about an innovative product that you would like to enter into the competition.

We're a growing tech company based in the US that is looking for new ideas for tech products to help with the health of twentysomethings like you! Is there a product that you or your friends could really benefit from? Whatever your ideas, we're looking for the most interesting ones!

The winning product will be developed by our team, and you will get hands-on experience of watching your ideas develop. Please submit all entries by April 1.

**Good luck!**

**B** **IN PAIRS** Work together to come up with your ideas for the competition entry.

**C** Present your ideas to each other as a class. Choose a winner.

**LIFE SKILLS** critical literacy

**A** **Read the definition of critical literacy. Why is being critically literate an important skill?**

Critical literacy describes a person's ability to understand and question the attitudes and beliefs that are part of any written (or spoken) text. Texts are produced for a particular audience by people who hold particular opinions. Being critically literate means that the reader (or listener) is able to understand the values of the writer and determine who the intended audience is.

**B** **IN GROUPS Look at this list of common medical beliefs and advice. Check the ones you think are medically accurate. Why might people give others this advice?**

1 ☐ To stay hydrated, you should drink at least eight glasses of water per day.
2 ☐ Sitting up straight helps avoid back problems.
3 ☐ You should wait half an hour after eating before going swimming.
4 ☐ Drinking milk strengthens your bones.
5 ☐ You shouldn't crack your knuckles because it can give you arthritis.
6 ☐ Reading in poor light can damage your eyesight.

**C** 🔊 **3.05 Read these texts and identify where they come from. Do you trust the medical information? Why or why not? Share your opinions with a member of your group.**

**1**  We all recognize and **accept** the importance of staying hydrated. Medical experts recommend that we drink at least eight glasses of water per day in order to stay happy and healthy. So why H20 Water? What **distinguishes** our water from other bottled water is that our water is naturally filtered and bottled at the source. Do your body a favor and always insist on H20 Water.

**2** All superheroes have to be healthy and strong. Milk is an excellent source of many important vitamins and minerals, including calcium, which your bones need to stay strong. So when your mom says to drink your milk, you can safely **assume** that mom knows what's best for her little hero. Milk—your secret superpower!

**3**

# I'm Becoming My Dad!!

DECEMBER 15 - 11:24

 < **26K** SHARES

I knew this day would come—I'm becoming my dad! The other day, I was at the beach with my kids, and we'd just finished our lunch. They wanted to run straight back to the ocean, but I heard myself saying, "You have to wait half an hour after eating before you can swim again." I **recall** my dad telling me that when I was a kid, and who am I to **reject** his advice?

**4**

## Knuckle Cracking— We've Cracked It!

The *Medical Myths* team is happy to **debunk** what your family has been telling you for years. Despite what they say, it is not true that cracking your knuckles leads to arthritis. A California doctor named Donald Unger cracked the knuckles of his left hand at least twice a day but didn't crack the knuckles on his right hand. At the end of the experiment—which lasted 50 years—there was no sign of arthritis in either hand. Myth debunked!

**D** **Discuss the questions as a class.**

1 Which products are promoted as healthy, and how do you know if they are really good for you?
2 What medical advice do families often tell children? What reasons might they have for giving them that advice?
3 How can you know if you should trust the information you read or hear?
4 In what other areas of work or study do you think using critical literacy skills is useful?

 **MAKE IT DIGITAL**

Research online for other common health or medical myths. Investigate where these myths may have come from. Prepare a fact sheet for other students with evidence that debunks these myths.

## VOCABULARY verns of thought

**A** Choose the word or phrase from LIFE SKILLS C that has a similar meaning to the word in bold.

| | | | |
|---|---|---|---|
| **1** | assume | **a** think without proof | **b** know to be true |
| **2** | accept | **a** believe | **b** argue |
| **3** | reject | **a** forget something | **b** refuse to accept something as true |
| **4** | debunk | **a** prove to be false | **b** prove to be true |
| **5** | recall | **a** remember | **b** understand |
| **6** | distinguish | **a** refuse to believe something | **b** notice the difference between |

## THINKING SKILL analyzing

**A** Read this information about how to analyze. In what other situations might you be asked to analyze something?

---

### Question:

I've been asked to "analyze" a text, but what does that mean?

### Dr. Simon Keyes responds:

It means that you need to study the text in detail in order to be able to identify what the main ideas, important themes, or arguments are. You may also be required to say whether you agree with a particular point or not and to give examples from the text to support your opinions.

 like |  dislike

---

**B** **IN PAIRS** Look at the photo. Can you do this? Discuss why you think some people are able to do this and some are not.

**C** Read this extract from an old biology textbook on genetics. Do you think it's accurate? Use a medical dictionary or go online to find out more up-to-date information on the topic. Then analyze the text.

### Genetics: The Basics

As Alfred Sturtevant has shown in a recent paper, the ability to curl one's tongue is an example of a genetic trait. This means that humans have inherited the ability to do this from their parents, and it is therefore not something that they can learn to do over time. Between 65% and 81% of the population can curl one or both sides of their tongues, and the ability is more common in women than in men. Tongue curling is an example of a Mendelian trait. Other examples include color blindness, dimples, and freckles.

**D** Write a checklist of the steps you took in order to analyze the text.

**E** **IN GROUPS** Share your checklists. Who followed the same steps as you?

## 🗨 MEDIATION **CONFIDENT COMMUNICATOR** communicating between cultures

**A** **Look at the photos. Which of these medical practices are used in your country? How effective do you think they are?**

Tai Chi: a traditional Chinese exercise program

herbal medicines: natural herbs for treating medical conditions

conventional medicine: manufactured medication and surgery

**B** 🔊 **3.06 Listen to these doctors talking about the types of medical practices they employ. Decide whether you agree or disagree with the opinions they express.**

Speaker 1: strongly agree / agree / disagree / strongly disagree
Speaker 2: strongly agree / agree / disagree / strongly disagree
Speaker 3: strongly agree / agree / disagree / strongly disagree
Speaker 4: strongly agree / agree / disagree / strongly disagree

**C** **IN PAIRS** Compare your opinions from **B** and give reasons and examples where possible.

**D** **Imagine that speakers from B were attending the same medical conference. Check which of the following strategies you think they would need to employ in order to communicate effectively.**

1 ☐ Show an appreciation and understanding of different perspectives and ideas, e.g., I don't agree with [person's name] completely, but I think that's a really good argument.
2 ☐ Encourage all participants to contribute to the discussion, e.g., Do you want to add anything to that, [person's name]?
3 ☐ Clarify any misunderstandings or miscommunications, e.g., So, let me just outline what I think [person's name] meant by that …
4 ☐ Discuss cultural similarities and differences, e.g., That doesn't happen in [my country], but I'd definitely like to learn more about it.
5 ☐ Adapt ideas or beliefs based on shared knowledge, e.g., I can understand why you might think that, but have you considered …

**E** **IN PAIRS** You are going to role-play an informal discussion between people at an international conference on different global medical practices. The title of the conference is "Different Medical Practices Around the World: What We Can Learn From One Another." Follow the instructions and do the role-play. Use strategies to communicate effectively and the phrases from **C** to help you.

Student A: You practice alternative medicine. You use alternative therapies to treat your patients, including acupuncture, massage, and herbal medicine. You think these methods are much more effective in treating people than conventional methods are. You want to encourage more people to learn about the benefits of alternative therapies.

Student B: You are a conventional medical practitioner. You are attending the conference because you strongly believe that conventional medicine is the best and most scientifically advanced way to treat a range of medical problems. You are very skeptical of the benefits of alternative medicine, but you want to find out more about it.

**F** **IN GROUPS** Discuss the questions.

1 How easy was it to communicate ideas to someone with a very different perspective from your own?
2 Do you think the culture that you come from determines the perspectives you have on a topic?

## VOCABULARY review

SCORE: / 10

A Complete the text with a word from the box in the correct form.

> affect   antibiotics   deprive   eliminate   infection   limbs   organs   recover   respond   wounds

Penicillin, or the active ingredient in most **1** _____, was first discovered in 1928, although the ancient Egyptians applied moldy bread and plant extracts to **2** _____ as a treatment against **3** _____. When the first commercially available medication went on sale, it came to be seen as a "wonder drug" for its ability to help people who were **4** _____ from injury. In the beginning, it was frequently used to heal injured soldiers who had lost **5** _____ on the battlefields of World War II or who were **6** _____ by gangrene, a terrible condition where the skin and tissue of the body is **7** _____ of blood and dies. While antibiotics have many advantages, they can have serious side effects including damage to **8** _____ caused by too much exposure to the bacteria. Our overuse of them has meant that some bacteria are now antibiotic resistant and can no longer be **9** _____. Ironically, our bodies inability to **10** _____ to these bacteria poses one of the most serious global risks to health.

## GRAMMAR review

SCORE: / 10

A Choose the correct option to complete the text.

**1 Although** / **In spite of** influenza (or "the flu" as it is usually known) is a serious illness, people in the past thought that it was caused by exposure to cold or wet weather. Nowadays, however, it is known that influenza is caused by the spread of viruses. **2 Despite the fact** / **Even though** the symptoms are often the same, influenza is far more dangerous than the common cold, largely because the viruses that cause it can change, or mutate. **3 In order to** / **So that** understand how these viruses are spread, the World Health Organization recognizes four types of influenza. Types A and B are known as "seasonal epidemics," **4 in order to** / **despite** the fact that they can occur at any time of year. Type C is a mild form and is not considered dangerous, and Type D occurs mostly in cattle. Data from the Centers for Disease Control and Prevention show that in the US alone, every year around 36,000 people die of influenza and over 200,000 are admitted to the hospital. **5 Even though** / **So as to** prevent the spread of influenza, people are encouraged to get the flu vaccination once a year.

B Complete the sentences with the correct form of the verbs in parentheses.

1 You _____ (have) the flu now if you _____ (not have) the vaccination.
2 If I _____ (study) for all my exams, I _____ (be) in medical school now.
3 Daryl _____ (not receive) any money after the accident if he _____ (not get) his car insured every year.
4 If the doctor _____ (not be) such a busy person, she _____ (be) happy to see you.
5 We _____ (be) on vacation now if you _____ (remember) the tickets!

> 16–20 correct: You can use dependent prepositions, medical terms, and verbs of thought.
> You can use mixed conditionals and clauses of contrast and purpose.
> 0–15 correct: Look again at the Vocabulary and Grammar sections in the unit.

TOTAL SCORE: / 20

## EXAM SKILLS  READING Scan a test for easier questions

Choose *True* or *False*.

1 It is helpful to scan questions for key words.                                    True / False
2 It is important to understand every single word in questions.        True / False
3 It is a good use of time to answer the easiest questions first.        True / False

> Go to Exams Skills on page 132–133 to learn how to scan questions to decide which to answer first.

# The World We Build

## WHAT DO YOU ALREADY KNOW?

**1 IN GROUPS** Think about these different features of a modern city or town. Which features do you think are the most important? Are there any features you might add?

- hospital
- office buildings
- parks
- schools
- roads
- waterways

## THINK AND PREPARE

**2** Decide whether you agree or disagree with this statement.

*The design of a city is ultimately what shapes the lives of its residents.*

**3 IN GROUPS** Prepare a panel discussion on the importance of urban design. Some members of your group will be experts on the panel and explain the role that urban planning plays. Other members of your group will be members of the community. Consider these points:

- the most important features of a city or town
- how design affects a resident's life
- how design does not affect a resident's life

**VIDEO** Watch the video as you prepare to hold a panel discussion and find out how to handle questions from the audience.

## SPEAK YOUR MIND

**4** Hold your panel discussion for the class.

### In this unit, you will …

- discuss the pros and cons of planned communities and compare plans for sustainable buildings.
- focus on Mediation: simplify information.
- focus on Thinking Skills: symbolizing.
- read about sustainable architecture.
- learn about decision-making to evaluate plans.
- read about having a global perspective and the professions that use this skill.

### LIFE SKILLS decision-making

**A** Read the definition of decision-making. What decisions do you need to make, and who do those decisions affect?

Decision-making is the ability to identify the pros and cons of the different options available. Every area of professional life requires making decisions, and there are always positive and negative results of choosing one option over another. The best decision-makers are able to calmly consider how their decision will affect everyone concerned and be confident in the decision they make.

**B** **IN PAIRS** Look at these two different designs for a planned community and identify the possible pros and cons of each design.

**1** Plan of a city based on a grid design (Washington, DC, US)

Pros: _____

Cons: _____

**2** Plan of a city based on a curvilinear design (Brasilia, Brazil)

Pros: _____

Cons: _____

**C** 4.01 Listen to a lecture describing two different designs for a planned community. In your notebook, list the pros and cons of each design mentioned by the speaker.

> **GLOSSARY**
>
> **navigate (v):** to find and follow a path through a difficult place

**D** **IN GROUPS** Discuss the questions.

**1** Which design would you decide to use if you could redesign your town or city?

**2** How many people would be affected by this decision? What difference could this decision make to their lives?

**3** What possible problems are there with using pros and cons to make a decision?

**MAKE IT DIGITAL**

Research the designs of different cities online. Identify which design planners used, and decide if that was the best design to use. Present your findings and decision to the class.

## VOCABULARY urban areas

**A** Complete the image with words from the box.

### 1 Urban _____

highway
infrastructure
pedestrian
subway
tunnel
underpass

2 _____
3 _____
4 _____
5 _____
6 _____

**B** Describe the urban infrastructure of the area where you live. How could it be improved?

## GRAMMAR inverted conditionals

**A** Read these examples from LIFE SKILLS **C** and answer the questions.

**1** Should they decide to go for a grid pattern, it will produce the following benefits. _____

**2** Had they used a different street layout, it would have been more difficult to design such a good system. _____

**3** Were you to use a grid system in an area with a lot of hills, you would end up with some very steep streets. _____

- Is the word order of the first part of the sentence like a question or a statement? _____

- Do these examples sound formal or informal? _____

**B** Label the examples (1–3) from GRAMMAR **A** with the name of the inverted conditional.

first    second    third

**C** Write a word or short phrase to complete each sentence in GRAMMAR **B**.

**1** Inverted conditionals are used in _____ speech and writing.

**2** Inverted first conditionals begin with _____ instead of *If … should*.

**3** Inverted second conditionals begin with _____ instead of *If … were*.

**4** Inverted third conditionals begin with _____ instead of *If … had*.

For more practice, go to page 162.

**D** Complete the inverted conditionals for each situation in your notebook, as in the example.

*Urban planners will hold public meetings when local residents object to their plans. (Should)*

*Should local residents object to their plans, urban planners will hold public meetings.*

**1** A grid system will work better if public transit is a priority. (Should)

**2** It would be easier to navigate our city if we had a grid system. (Were)

**3** Many cities would build a subway system if it were affordable. (Were)

**4** If the original planners had known how big Washington, DC, would become, they might have made different decisions. (Had)

**5** If the council decides that pedestrian access is important, we will conduct a feasibility study. (Should)

# PRONUNCIATION /ʌ/, /ʊ/, and /uː/

**A** 🔊 **4.02 Listen to these words and write each one in the correct category.**

> construct  consume  food  luxury  should  subway
> super  tunnel  underpass  wood  would

**1** /ʌ/ *cut, come,* _____

**2** /ʊ/ *look, put,* _____

**3** /uː/ *cool, school,* _____

**B** **Practice saying the sentences. Pay attention to the vowel sounds.**

A new tunnel would be a good idea.
Wood is sometimes a luxury construction material.
It's not cool to consume too much food.
We should use buses more and use cars less.

# SPEAKING

For more speaking practice, go to page 149.

**A** **IN PAIRS Read about this planned community. Discuss what you would like or dislike about living there.**

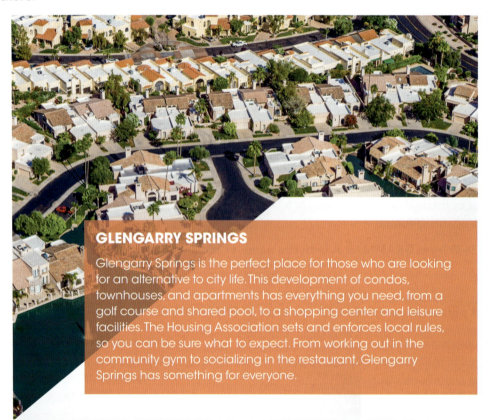

**GLENGARRY SPRINGS**

Glengarry Springs is the perfect place for those who are looking for an alternative to city life. This development of condos, townhouses, and apartments has everything you need, from a golf course and shared pool, to a shopping center and leisure facilities. The Housing Association sets and enforces local rules, so you can be sure what to expect. From working out in the community gym to socializing in the restaurant, Glengarry Springs has something for everyone.

**B** **IN PAIRS Discuss the pros and cons of living in a place such as Glengarry Springs. Make notes of your ideas and then share them with the class.**

A: *I think there would be a number of pros. For example, you have all the infrastructure you need, such as a shopping center and leisure facilities.*

B: *Yeah, I guess so. If I were living there, though, I might find it too quiet. I love the noise and activity of the city.*

A: *Maybe you could take the subway into the city when you wanted that. Another pro is …*

# READING

**A** **IN GROUPS** Discuss what traditional and alternative sources there are for power, heating, and lighting for people to use in their houses.

**B** 🔊 4.03 See which of your examples of alternative sources from **A** are mentioned in this poster for an architectural competition.

## Sustainable Architecture Competition

The State of Alaska is looking for proposals for an ambitious new project in Anchorage. The competition is open to all undergraduate architecture students across the United States, not only in the State of Alaska.

The architecture student (or team of students) will design a sustainable house for the modern family. The construction and the use of the house must aim to have the smallest carbon footprint possible (a calculation of the carbon use for the building and use of the house must be included in the proposal). Finally, the design must be scalable—it will be used to create 120 new homes in a residential area of Anchorage!

### Proposals must consider:

#### Power
In order not to rely on any national power sources, the house will need to produce its own energy locally. Possible sources for energy could include **solar panels** on the roof or outside of the house, or the use of **micro wind turbines**. National sources such as rivers cannot be considered for power use in the design.

#### Heating
The house must use natural sources of heat for the majority of its heating. **Solar thermal collectors** can be used to heat water for the house. However, it is important to consider that Anchorage has a long winter season. Consequently, it will be important to include alternative heat sources such as **geothermal heating** under the house.

#### Lighting
Annually, there are different amounts of daylight in Anchorage, ranging from the shortest day of around 5.5 hours to the longest day of 22 hours. For this reason, it is important to include different options for lighting. **Smart lighting**, which instantly reacts to the light outside, could be used, but designs that focus on **daylighting** instead of the use of artificial light will be preferred.

#### Carbon Footprint
The design should include a number of different ways to reduce the carbon footprint of the house. These could include **green roofs** for carbon capture or **rainwater harvesting** to use as many of the natural resources as possible. In the winter in Anchorage, there can sometimes be issues with frozen pipes, so this needs to be included in the proposal.

#### Competition Deadline
The deadline for proposals is midday, October 2, and all proposals and the calculations for carbon use must be submitted via email.

### GLOSSARY

**carbon footprint** (n): the amount of carbon dioxide produced by a building, person, etc.
**scalable** (adj): describes a system or design that continues to work well when used on a large scale or by many people
**sustainable** (adj): using methods that do not damage the environment

**C** **IN PAIRS READING SKILL—Identify reasons** Read the poster again and discuss the questions.

1 Why is it important that the design for the house is scalable?
2 Why does the house need to produce its own energy locally?
3 Why should the house include alternative heat and light sources?

**D** **IN GROUPS** Discuss if any of these features of sustainable architecture are used in buildings in your local area. Why or why not?

# VOCABULARY sustainable architecture

**A** Complete the definitions with the phrases in the box.

| daylighting | geothermal heating | green roof | micro wind turbine |
|---|---|---|---|
| rainwater harvesting | smart lighting | solar panel | solar thermal collector |

1 _____ : the storage of water that falls onto a house in tanks

2 _____ : the use of as much light as possible from natural sources

3 _____ : a small wheel that produces electricity when turned by a flow of air

4 _____ : a lighting system that adapts to the movement of people or the amount of daylight available

5 _____ : a feature on the roof of a building that uses the light from the sun to produce electricity

6 _____ : a heating system that pulls heat up from the ground into the house

7 _____ : a term used when plants are grown on the top of a house to help with carbon capture

8 _____ : a machine that heats water or air with the natural heat of the sun

⭐ **MAKE IT YOURS**

How could buildings in your area become sustainable? What other features can make buildings sustainable? Look up other words related to sustainable architecture.

**B** **IN PAIRS** Discuss the advantages and disadvantages of each of these features.

# GRAMMAR review of adverbs

**A** Match each group of adverbs to the correct description.

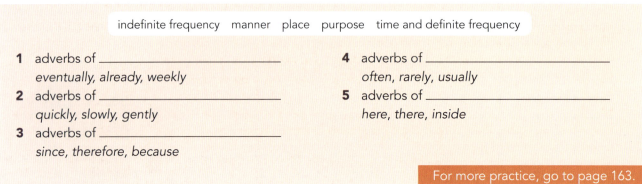

indefinite frequency   manner   place   purpose   time and definite frequency

1 adverbs of _____
*eventually, already, weekly*

2 adverbs of _____
*quickly, slowly, gently*

3 adverbs of _____
*since, therefore, because*

4 adverbs of _____
*often, rarely, usually*

5 adverbs of _____
*here, there, inside*

For more practice, go to page 163.

**B** Find and underline one example of each type of adverb in READING B.

**C** Complete the text with words from the box.

always   automatically   never   often   since   therefore

The Crystal, a building in London, England, has a system that is
**1** _____ on around the clock and that constantly
checks the amount of daylight available and the presence of
people around the building. Heating and cooling are controlled
**2** _____. **3** _____, the use of energy
is very efficient. Energy comes from ground-source heat pumps, which
heat water deep in the earth. The building **4** _____
receives an energy bill **5** _____ natural sources provide
all of its energy needs. It **6** _____ rains in England, so
the Crystal collects rainwater to filter and use throughout the building.
The Crystal is one of the world's most sustainable buildings.

# THINKING SKILL symbolizing

**A** **IN PAIRS** Read about symbolizing and discuss when it may be important in your career.

Symbolizing is the ability to express ideas using images. It involves understanding the most important aspects of ideas and translating those aspects visually. Some symbols may be personal, for example when taking notes. Other symbols are more universal (e.g., a heart may symbolize love) and can help to communicate ideas to other people.

**B** Look at these logos with your partner. Choose words and phrases from the box that express what each logo symbolizes. You will not use all the words.

environmentally friendly   fun   high quality   high-tech   inexpensive   luxury   modern   reliable

**C** **IN PAIRS** You have been asked to design a logo for a sustainable architecture company, Green Architects. Design your logo and explain how different aspects symbolize the company.

# SPEAKING

For more speaking practice, go to page 149.

**A** Design a sustainable home. Make notes in your notebook on what you could do to make each of these aspects of the building sustainable.

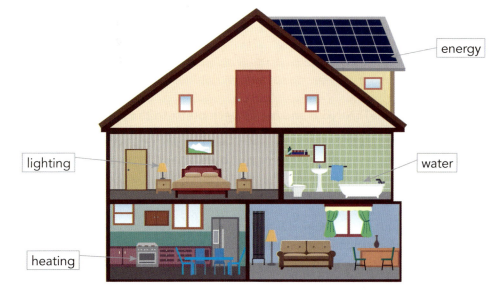

**B** **IN PAIRS** Compare your plans. Explain to each other how your building works and what makes it sustainable.

A: *First of all, the house is built of stone. It's a sustainable material, and it's available locally.*

B: *Good idea. What about energy use?*

A: *It's controlled automatically. There's a computer system that monitors energy use and turns off parts of the house that aren't being used at that moment.*

## LISTENING

**A** **IN PAIRS** Discuss which of these buildings you would prefer to see more of in your city's downtown area. Explain why.

**B** 🔊 **4.04 LISTENING SKILL—Listen for agreement and disagreement** Listen to this interview and check (✓) the points the speakers agree on.

**1** ☐ It's important to attract new businesses to the city.
**2** ☐ It will be necessary to build more roads in the downtown area.
**3** ☐ Cost is the most important factor in the plans.
**4** ☐ The appearance of the city skyline is important to residents.
**5** ☐ Employment is important to local people.

**C** Listen again and write a word or short phrase to complete the points each speaker makes.

Jade

**1** The city needs to _____ to do better than other cities in the area.
**2** Thomas's suggestion would take time and be _____.
**3** Residents want to see investment and the creation of _____.

Thomas

**4** Some investors are attracted by the _____ of the city.
**5** Jade's plan would affect the _____ of local residents.
**6** Jade's plan would attract _____ to the city.

## VOCABULARY verb prefixes *dis–*, *out–*, and *un–*

**A** Look at these sentences from **LISTENING B** and match each prefix to the correct meaning.

**1** If we are going to **out**perform other cities in the local area, we need to change and adapt. _____
**2** We should not **un**do the work that people in our city did in the past. _____
**3** Most of them **dis**like the appearance of modern skyscrapers. _____

**a** negative, not, opposite
**b** reverse an action
**c** more than, better than

**B** **IN PAIRS** Match the verb prefixes *dis–*, *out–*, and *un–* to the verbs below. Use a dictionary if necessary. One of the verbs has two possible prefixes.

| _____appoint | _____bid | _____cover | _____lock | _____please |
|---|---|---|---|---|
| _____associate | _____connect | _____live | _____number | _____tie |

💡 **MAKE IT REAL**

Verbs with these prefixes are excellent for formal writing and speaking.
In more informal contexts, people often use phrasal verbs like *let down* for *disappoint*, or *dig up* for *uncover*.

# WRITING an email proposal

**A** **IN PAIRS** Complete this brainstorm diagram with the suggestions and expected results from the email proposal for changing part of a local town.

| New Message | |
| --- | --- |
| To: Councilor Martins | Cc   Bcc |
| Subject: Old factory | |

**Dear Councilor Martins,**

As you know, the old factory on the edge of town has become a problem area in our community. The building is old, unattractive, and in a dangerous condition. I am writing to suggest a better way to use the space.

I propose that four new developments should be built on the site of the old factory. The first suggestion is a modern office building. Providing more office space will probably attract businesses to the area, and attracting businesses will create jobs. The second is a new shopping mall. The town has excellent local businesses but needs to attract money from global companies. Besides that, building a mall will probably be popular with residents.

The third suggestion is to build a play area for children and a leisure park for young people because this will promote sports and positive behavior among young people. Finally, building office space and a mall probably won't work without the right infrastructure so I propose that new roads are created that connect the town to the factory site. Recent studies have shown the population will increase, so the roads are necessary to reduce traffic.

Thank you for considering my proposal, and I look forward to your response.

Olivia Hancock

*Send*

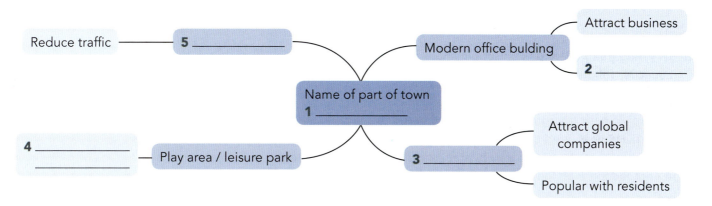

**B** In your notebook, write alternative ways to make the predictions in the email using the words given.

> Building a leisure park will promote positive behavior among young people. (likely)
> *Building a leisure park is likely to promote positive behavior among young people.*

1. Providing more office space will probably attract businesses. (likely)
2. Attracting businesses will create jobs. (sure)
3. Building a mall will probably be popular with residents. (expected)
4. Building office space and a mall probably won't work without the right infrastructure. (unlikely)
5. The population will increase so the roads are necessary to reduce traffic. (forecasted)

**C** **IN PAIRS** In your notebook, create a brainstorm diagram like the one in **A** for a part of your local area that needs to be developed.

**D** Write an email to your local councilor outlining your proposal for developing your local area. Use a variety of adjectives and verbs.

## 🗨 MEDIATION CONFIDENT COMMUNICATOR simplifying information

**A** Read the dialogue from a public meeting. Choose *True* or *False*.

Councilor: It's become clear to all of us on the city council that we need to redevelop the downtown area. I'd like to present some of our plans for that redevelopment now. Yes, I think we have a question at the back.

Resident: I'm sorry, but I really don't understand why the redevelopment is necessary. Could you explain that?

Councilor: Sure. First of all, it's important to know that other cities in the area are outperforming us. Put simply, they attract large businesses, and we don't. Were we to do nothing, we would fall further behind. So, as a result of that, we need to make our city more attractive to businesses. Does that make sense?

Resident: Yes, it does.

Councilor: To address that problem, we've tried offering financial incentives such as tax reductions, but it hasn't really worked. The reason for this is that we don't have the infrastructure that businesses need. They want modern office space and good transportation connections. We could build highways and improve the transportation links, but that would still leave the problem of not having enough suitable buildings. Therefore, we need to redevelop the whole downtown area. Is that any clearer?

Resident: Yes, thank you for the explanation.

| | |
|---|---|
| **1** The resident asks the councilor to explain the reasons for their plans. | True / False |
| **2** The councilor explains by breaking the argument down into small steps. | True / False |
| **3** The councilor uses linking phrases to connect the steps in the argument. | True / False |
| **4** The councilor checks the resident's understanding. | True / False |
| **5** The resident finds the councilor's explanation difficult to follow. | True / False |

**B** **IN PAIRS** Read these tips on simplifying information. Say where in the dialogue the councilor follows each tip.

In order to simplify information, it's a good idea to …
1 explain basic background facts that are relevant.
2 explain ideas using clear language.
3 present the information step by step, showing causes and effects.
4 get feedback on the other person's understanding.

**C** Choose which of the statements you agree with. In your notebook, list the reasons for your opinion.

Our city's main focus should be on attracting more businesses.
Our city's main focus should be on attracting more tourists.
Our city's main focus should be on improving the quality of life for residents.

**D** **IN GROUPS** Say which statement you have chosen and explain the reasons for your opinion. Use the tips in **B** to make your argument as clear as possible.

**E** Discuss the questions.

1 Did you find it easy to follow other people's arguments? Why or why not?
2 When might you need to simplify information in this way in your working life?

## VOCABULARY review

SCORE: / 10

**A** Complete each sentence with a word formed from the word in parentheses.

1 We need better _____ (structure) in this city to attract businesses.

2 I can't _____ (lock) the door to get in. Are you sure this is the right key?

3 Supporters of the new development _____ (number) opponents by two to one.

4 I don't want to _____ (appoint) you, but the council voted against your suggestion.

5 They've _____ (connect) the electricity because they're doing some work on the street.

**B** Choose the correct word.

1 Effective **daylighting** / **nightlighting** can significantly reduce the need for artificial lights.

2 We need to build more areas for **drivers** / **pedestrians** to walk around the city center.

3 Let's take the **highway** / **subway**. The train will be faster than driving across town.

4 We have a **solar panel** / **solar thermal collector** on the roof, which provides us with hot water all day long.

5 Many residents were **disliked** / **displeased** at the development plans.

## GRAMMAR review

SCORE: / 10

**A** Complete the paragraph with words from the box.

> already   easily   eventually   had   particularly   should   since   therefore   usually   were

1 _____ you to measure the temperature in a city and compare it with the area around the city, you would find that cities are 2 _____ hotter. This "urban heat island" effect is caused by the built environment. Roads and buildings are darker than natural areas, and 3 _____ they absorb more heat from the sun. After some time, they 4 _____ radiate that heat back, causing the temperature to rise, 5 _____ at night. The heat tends to stay in the area 6 _____ tall buildings prevent air from circulating 7 _____. 8 _____ city engineers want to solve this problem, there are a few things they can do. They can create buildings with green roofs using plants, and some cities are 9 _____ doing this. They can also paint roofs white, which means the roofs reflect heat and light. 10 _____ city engineers known about the problem decades ago, they might have designed buildings differently from the beginning.

> 16–20 correct: You can use the language of sustainable architecture and urban areas, and the verb prefixes *dis–*, *out–*, and *un–*.
> You can use inverted conditionals and adverbs.
> 0–15 correct: Look again at the Vocabulary and Grammar sections in the unit.

TOTAL SCORE: / 20

## SKILLS FOR PROS    Global Perspective

Read this statement. Do you agree?

### The only way to get to know another culture is to travel to that part of the world.

Turn to Skills for Pros on page 134.

# Our Changing Future

**WHAT DO YOU ALREADY KNOW?**

1 **IN GROUPS** Look at the picture. Discuss how you think the employment market will change in the future as more and more technology is introduced into the workplace. In your opinion, will the changes be positive or negative?

**THINK AND PREPARE**

2 Decide whether you agree or disagree with this statement.

*By the end of the 21st century, robots will do most of the jobs currently done by humans.*

3 **IN GROUPS** Prepare for a discussion on whether you think your career will be affected by the introduction of robots in the workplace. Make notes on your predictions about the changes and any recommendations you might have for people who work in your career. Consider these points:
- the balance of physical vs. mental tasks
- the creation of new jobs that do not currently exist
- the efficiency and cost of robots in comparison to people

**VIDEO**

Watch the video as you prepare to hold a discussion and find out how to keep the discussion on track.

**SPEAK YOUR MIND**

4 Have your discussion. Give reasons to support your predictions and your recommendations.

**In this unit, you will ...**

- predict the future of humanity and discuss daily life in the 22nd century.
- focus on Mediation: adapt language.
- focus on Thinking Skills: brainstorming.
- read about the practice of predicting the future.
- learn about global competence: think of solutions for global issues.
- practice your written exam skills by using reasons to support your opinions.

## READING

**A** As a class, discuss whether any of the inventions shown in these old postcards are similar to things that exist now. Then read the blog to find out which of the predictions are mentioned.

Postcards showing predictions about the 21st century made at the beginning of the 20th century

electric scrubber

electric education

robot barbers

### The Past and Far, Far Into the Future

👥 Followers

When you're thinking about the future, do you ever wonder about things like, for example, hair salons? Will hair stylists have disappeared by the 22nd century? Will people have started getting their hair cut by robots? This was actually one of the predictions that people made at the turn of the last century, from the 19th to the 20th century. Another prediction was that there would be electric education. This did not predict computer-based instruction or anything similar to what we have today; it predicted that books would be fed into a machine and the "knowledge" would be transferred electronically directly to students' brains! In 1900, there were a lot of predictions about what people thought would have happened by the year 2000, and some of the predictions seem very odd today!

Nevertheless, think of all the life-changing inventions that *did* occur in the 20th century. In 1900, none of these things existed: radio, TV, vacuum cleaners, airplanes, color photography, movies, frozen food, antibiotics, radar, and ballpoint pens. Cars had been invented, but almost no one had one until the mass production of the Model T in 1908. Of course, much later in the 20th century, we saw the development of microwave ovens, cell phones, digital watches, the internet, and many, many other things that we now use every day without thinking about what life would be like without them.

So what about the predictions being made now for life in the early 22nd century? Which of those might turn out to be accurate? For example, many people think that by the beginning of the next century, we will have **found a cure for** cancer, as well as for many other fatal diseases. Many people also say that we will have **landed on** another planet. Here are some further predictions for the early 22nd century:

- Language classes will have **become obsolete**. Instant translation programs will be so good that no one will need to speak any language but their own, and everyone will be able to talk to anyone in the world.
- Contact lenses will have **been upgraded** to give us superhuman eyesight. We'll be able to see great distances or see very tiny objects. We will have **done away with** glasses entirely.
- Nanorobots will have been implanted in everyone's bodies. They will fix damaged cells and protect us from many diseases.
- Virtual worlds will have become real. Because of computer-brain connections, people will be able to live in whatever type of world they choose.

Some of the predictions for the end of this century seem likely to happen, while others seem completely unrealistic. Anyway, it is probably safe to predict that by the end of the 21st century, people will not have stopped wanting new things to make their lives easier, better, or more interesting. Inventors will not have **run out of** ideas. Companies will not have **given up on** producing new products. What amazing new things will people have achieved 100 years from now? Will human organ transplants be done with organs created on 3D printers? Will scientists have figured out how to enable people to live forever? And if so, will laboratories produce enough food and fresh water for everyone? If we look at how the 20th century started and ended, as well as how we **made** so much **progress** in medicine and technology in just the first two decades of the 21st century, we can imagine that the possibilities for the end of the 22nd century are practically endless.

**B** 🔊 **5.01 READING SKILL—Identify main ideas** Read the blog again. Match the main ideas to the paragraphs.

1 Paragraph 1: _____
2 Paragraph 2: _____
3 Paragraph 3: _____
4 Paragraph 4: _____

**a** There are a number of predictions about achievements by the beginning of the 22nd century.
**b** Based on the number of achievements in the 20th century and the first two decades of the 21st century, it is logical to assume that there will be many major achievements by the beginning of the 22nd century.
**c** Some strange and inaccurate predictions were made about the 21st century.
**d** There were many major achievements in the 20th century.

**C** **IN GROUPS** Discuss whether you think the predictions for the 22nd century mentioned in the text will come true.

## GRAMMAR future perfect

**A** Look at the examples from **READING A** and choose the correct options to complete the rules.

> **Simple future**
> Because of computer-brain connections, people will be able to live in whatever type of world they choose.
> Will laboratories **produce** enough food and fresh water for everyone?
>
> **Future perfect**
> Will hair stylists **have disappeared** by the 22nd century?
> By the beginning of the next century, we **will have found a cure for** cancer, as well as for many other fatal diseases.
> Companies **will not have given up on** producing new products.
>
> 1 The simple future expresses an action or situation that …
>   **a** will happen or be true at or before a specific time in the future.
>   **b** will happen or be true at some point in the future.
> 2 The future perfect expresses an action or situation that …
>   **a** will happen or be true at or before a specific time in the future.
>   **b** will happen or be true at some point in the future.
> 3 The future perfect is formed with …
>   **a** *will/won't + have/has + simple past verb.*
>   **b** *will/won't + have + past participle verb.*
>
> For more practice, go to page 164.

**B** Complete the predictions with the correct forms of the verbs in parentheses.

1 By the year 2050, we _____ (create) a base on the moon.
2 They _____ (find) a cure for cancer very soon.
3 There _____ (not be) any hunger in the world in the future.
4 By the beginning of the next century, cars _____ (disappear).
5 We _____ (not solve) the problem of climate change by 2030.

**C** **IN PAIRS** Check your answers and say whether you agree with the predictions.

## VOCABULARY progress

**A** Write the base form of the verb phrases in bold in READING A next to the definitions.

1 _____: to come down to the Earth or another planet after being in the air

2 _____: to use all of something and not have any left

3 _____: to get rid of something

4 _____: to stop trying to make something happen

5 _____: to be no longer used because there is something newer and better

6 _____: to invent or discover a treatment for a disease

7 _____: to advance in the process of doing something

8 _____: to improve the quality of a product or service

⭐ **MAKE IT YOURS**

What areas of your life will be upgraded in the future? What aspects of your life will become obsolete? How else will your life change? Look up words that describe progress.

## SPEAKING

For more speaking practice, go to page 150.

**A** For each area below, write two predictions for things that you think people will have achieved by beginning of the next century.

Health and medicine

_____

_____

Sports and athletes

_____

_____

Transportation

_____

_____

Environment

_____

_____

**B** **IN GROUPS** Share your predictions and say whether you think they will have come true by the beginning of the 22nd century.

## LISTENING

**A**   **IN PAIRS** Make a list of resources the world will need in the future. Why do you think the world will need them? How will we be able to get all the resources we need?

**B**   🔊 **5.02** Listen to a science podcast on ways to find the resources the world will need in the future. Complete the notecards.

---

Resource = minerals, e.g., gold and silver

Problem: Minerals may run out soon

Used to produce environmentally
   friendly technology, e.g.,
  **1** _____

Sulfides contain: copper, zinc, lead,
  **2** _____

---

Resource = chemicals, e.g., halichondrin B
Problem: Need new sources of **3** _____
Found in animals and plants in the ocean, e.g.,
  **4** _____

Resource = sustainable food
Problem: Producing food relies on **5** _____
Food grown in a combination of pure water and nutrients
from **6** _____ shells

---

**C**   🔊 **5.03 LISTENING SKILL—Understand reference** Listen to the excerpts from the podcast. Decide what the phrases with "that" refer to.

**1**   "That's difficult to believe, right?" refers to how long …
  **a**   Steve and Tom have been making the podcast.     **b**   Steve and Tom have been friends.

**2**   "But why is that a problem?" refers to …
  **a**   the theme of the show.     **b**   our need for minerals and precious metals.

**3**   "But that isn't all we find in the ocean, is it?" refers to the source of …
  **a**   minerals.     **b**   medicine.

**4**   "That means we need new sources of medicine." refers to our need for new sources of medicine …
  **a**   after centuries looking all over the Earth.     **b**   in the ocean.

**5**   "I'd say that was impossible!" refers to producing food …
  **a**   in a desert.     **b**   without fresh water.

## THINKING SKILL brainstorming

**A**   **IN PAIRS** Look at different ways to brainstorm a topic. Do you ever use any of these methods? Do you know any other methods?

make a chart       make a word map       free writing

**B**   **IN PAIRS** Think about the future. How do you think everyday life will be different (e.g., food, work, education)? Choose one of the methods in **A** and work with a partner to brainstorm your ideas.

**C**   **IN GROUPS** Share your ideas with another pair and discuss the questions.

**1**   Did you use the same methods to think of ideas?
**2**   Which method of brainstorming worked best for this topic and why?

# VOCABULARY  adverbs of attitude

**A** Write the number of the adverb next to the corresponding underlined phrase.

| | | | |
|---|---|---|---|
| **1** frankly | **3** honestly | **5** optimistically | **7** admittedly |
| **2** apparently | **4** arguably | **6** realistically | **8** negatively |

It drives me crazy when people think they are being positive about the planet and all they do is talk about the problems that we are facing. OK, <u>I have to agree that</u> _____ there are a lot of problems and, yes, <u>you could argue that</u> _____ there are some that will be difficult to solve. But we have found so many solutions already! <u>To tell you the truth</u> _____, I believe we need to focus on acting positively. <u>At the risk of being rude</u> _____, people who <u>appear to</u> _____ have a deep understanding of problems like our lack of food or fresh water are often exactly the same people who have not researched the solutions that exist. These people just spend their time talking <u>in a critical way</u> _____ about all the things we are doing wrong instead of going out there and helping. <u>The real situation is that</u> _____, there will always be problems that humans have to face, but I believe that if we think and act <u>in a positive way</u> _____, we have much more of a chance of finding the solutions we need.

> 💡 **MAKE IT REAL**
>
> In instant messages, people often use letters representing short phrases to introduce their opinion or attitude on a topic. Examples include *TBH* (*to be honest*) and *IMO* (*in my opinion*).

**B** **IN PAIRS** Check your answers and say whether you agree with the writer.

# PRONUNCIATION  adverbs of attitude

**A** 🔊 **5.04 IN PAIRS** Listen and underline the stressed syllable in each adverb. Then take turns reading the sentences in **VOCABULARY A** aloud.

| | | | |
|---|---|---|---|
| frankly | honestly | optimistically | admittedly |
| apparently | arguably | realistically | negatively |

# GRAMMAR  future perfect progressive

**A** Look at the examples and choose the correct options to complete the rules.

> **Future perfect**
> We will have run out of our supply of gold by as early as 2050.
>
> **Future perfect progressive**
> By the end of this year, these drugs will have been helping cancer patients for over 10 years.

**1** The future perfect expresses an action that …
  **a** will be completed at or before a specific time in the future.
  **b** will start happening at some point in the future.

**2** The future perfect progressive expresses an action or situation that …
  **a** will be in progress at some point in the future.
  **b** will have been in progress for a period of time before a specific time in the future.

**3** The future perfect progressive is formed with …
  **a** *will/won't + have + been + –ing* verb.
  **b** *will/won't + have + been + past participle verb.*

For more practice, go to page 165.

**B** In your notebook, answer the questions with your own information.

1 At the end of this course, how long will you have been studying English?

2 By the end of this year, how long will you have been living in your house?

3 By the time you retire, how long will you have been working? If you are not working yet, estimate from the age you think you will start working.

**C** **IN PAIRS** Compare your answers.

## WRITING an opinion post

**A** **IN PAIRS** Read this opinion post. Write *example*, *opinion*, *reason*, or *evidence*, depending on the function of each sentence in the paragraph about antibiotics.

Sentence 1: _____    Sentence 3: _____

Sentence 2: _____    Sentence 4: _____

### A Common Mistake When Predicting the Future

When people make predictions about the future, they often only focus on one aspect of future life without considering the evidence. Here are a couple of examples of what I mean.

**1** Many people say we won't be able to control new kinds of bacteria because of our overuse of antibiotics. **2** However, I don't think this will happen. **3** After penicillin was used in World War II, it was used for all kinds of infections in both humans and farm animals. Now around 70% of antibiotics in the US are used for animals, and antibiotics are controlled by the Food and Drug Administration. **4** If we are taking steps to control our use of antibiotics now, why will this be a problem in the future?

Another popular prediction is that robots will take our jobs and there will not be enough work for humans. This will probably not be true. Similar predictions were made during the Industrial Revolution in the 19th century, but if you look at the poverty figures, you can see that they did not come true. According to the World Bank, in 1820 almost 90% of the world's population was living in poverty, but in 2015, world poverty was at 10%. Currently, the creation of new technologies leads to the creation of new jobs, and I predict that this will continue in the future.

As you can see, if you look at current evidence, the predictions for the future do not seem as dramatic.

**B** **IN PAIRS** With your partner, read the paragraph about robots in the opinion post and look for opinions, examples, reasons, and evidence.

**C** Write an opinion post with your opinions on predictions about problems in the future. Include examples, reasons, and evidence.

**D** **IN PAIRS** Read each other's opinion posts. Say whether you agree with your partner's ideas.

## SPEAKING

For more speaking practice, go to page 150.

**A** Read the predictions about everyday life in the year 3000. Check (✓) the ones you think will be true or partly true.

- ☐ There will be no more domestic animals. People will have been buying robot pets for at least 400 years, so we won't need domestic animals.
- ☐ For many years, computers and machines will have been doing all the jobs that people don't like, so everyone will only do creative and fun jobs.
- ☐ Since about 2300, people will have been living in flying mobile homes and traveling to several different planets.

**B** **IN GROUPS** Discuss the predictions in A. Make your own predictions about daily life in the year 3000.

*By the year 3000, I think it will have become normal for everybody to have robot pets.*

## LIFE SKILLS global competence

**A** **IN PAIRS** Read the definition of global competence. Identify which global issues you both consider to be the most important.

Global competence is the ability to investigate the world by understanding and getting interested in issues of global importance. It involves sharing knowledge, listening to different perspectives, and forming opinions and conclusions based on factual evidence.

**B** 🔊 **5.05** Check (✓) the things that you think are aspects of population change. Read the article and check your answers.

- ⬭ overpopulation of some countries and underpopulation of others
- ⬭ people moving from small towns to large cities
- ⬭ more old people and fewer young people
- ⬭ more people living alone
- ⬭ more working women

## Trends in Population in the 21st Century

There are a number of trends that show that by the late 21st century, some very important demographic changes will have taken place. The overall trend in world population is growth. According to the World Bank, world population is growing at about 1.1% annually, which means that the population increases by about 83 million people every year. The percentage of growth is less than it was in the 1960s, but because world population is now over seven billion, the population increase in actual numbers is greater than ever before. The vast majority of population growth is happening in developing countries. This means that countries that may already experience a lack of food, fresh water, educational opportunities, and job opportunities will have even more problems in the future. They may not **have the ability to** survive if they do not get help. To what extent other countries **have the obligation to** help developing countries will become an even more urgent question as populations increase.

Demographers predict the opposite problem for some countries. They say that the populations of Germany, Italy, Japan, Russia, and South Korea will have decreased greatly by the end of this century. Other countries that are currently growing, like the US, Canada, Australia, and France, will stop growing by the end of the century if there are not many new immigrants to those countries.

Other trends predicted by demographers also raise important questions:

**1** There will be an increasingly older population in developed countries. This will mean that there are fewer people in the workforce and more people using social services for the elderly. Will there be a **need to** raise taxes to help pay for those social services?

**2** There will be more working women. This means that women and families will **have a chance to** be more economically secure, but it also means that more people will be competing for fewer jobs as technology replaces humans in the workplace. How will enough jobs be created for everyone?

**3** More people will be living alone. Because of the very large older population, many elderly people will live alone after a spouse dies. Also, young people are increasingly mobile and often live alone when they move to a new city. What kinds of problems might this cause in housing and mental health?

**4** There will be much larger urban populations and smaller rural populations because of a change from agriculture-based to technology-based economies. What kinds of problems will this cause for cities, and how will we produce enough food if there is less agriculture?

Many of these issues already exist, and they will become more important as populations grow and change. We **have a responsibility to** think about the questions and possible solutions now. If we don't **make an attempt to** prepare for the future, we will have bigger problems than we have now.

### GLOSSARY

**demographer (n):** a person who studies populations
**spouse (n):** a husband or a wife

**C** IN PAIRS **Look at the four problems mentioned by demographers in the article. Match each one to a suggestion for managing the problem. In your notebook, write at least one more suggestion for each problem.**

a Adapt education systems and learning according to changes in the workplace. _____

b Change business practices and systems to include older workers. _____

c Encourage companies to move to smaller, more rural areas and find ways to improve food technology. _____

d Involve architects and urban planners in creating innovations in housing and communities. _____

**D** IN GROUPS **Discuss the questions and share your ideas.**

1 Compare your suggestions. Are these realistic, workable solutions?

2 Why is it important to have an awareness of global issues such as population growth?

3 Do you see any evidence of these problems where you live, work, or study?

**MAKE IT DIGITAL**

Find several interesting predictions for global demographics. Discuss which predictions might affect your country. Have a discussion on the best way to deal with those issues.

## VOCABULARY verb + noun + infinitive

**A** **Match the parts to make sentences. Use the phrases in bold in LIFE SKILLS B.**

1 Some people say there is a **need to** make _____

2 Some people **have the ability to** tolerate _____

3 I think the government **has the obligation to** take _____

4 I hope someday I **have a chance to** live _____

5 We have to **make an attempt to** plan _____

6 I believe that rich countries **have a responsibility to** help _____

a big changes in society every few years.

b in another country.

c care of all senior citizens.

d developing countries.

e high levels of stress in their jobs.

f for demographic changes to avoid problems in the future.

**B** **Complete the paragraphs with the phrases in bold in A. Make changes to the tense where necessary.**

I like where I live, and even if I won the lottery and I suddenly **1** _____ move to another city, I wouldn't. I don't think there **2** _____ make constant changes in my life.

Everyone should **3** _____ develop positive habits that can benefit society. We should think about others and not just about ourselves. I am confident that this society **4** _____ take care of everyone if we decide to do it.

To what extent does the world **5** _____ take care of its citizens? I believe that countries with resources should sign an agreement that means they **6** _____ provide food for people in countries without resources.

**C** IN PAIRS **Write at least one sentence expressing your ideas using each phrase in bold in A.**

1 _____

2 _____

3 _____

4 _____

5 _____

6 _____

🗨 MEDIATION **CONFIDENT COMMUNICATOR** adapting language

**A** Match a speaker's original language (1–3) to another speaker's simpler adaptation of the language (a–c).

**Speaker 1**

**1** "I think the major problem in my country related to population change is **scarcity** of resources, especially water, partly caused by population growth." _____

**2** "There is already water **scarcity**, and it will have reached **crisis level** in just a few years if there is **a failure to address it**." _____

**3** "Without water, people will no longer be able to survive in rural areas, and there will be a **mass migration** to the cities. City governments will not be able to provide services for so many residents—services like transportation, garbage collection, and hospitals. The result of all of this will be more **poverty**." _____

**Speaker 2**

**a** "He said there is already a lack of water, and it will be an enormous problem a few years from now if they don't do something about it."

**b** "If there isn't enough water in rural areas, more and more people will move to the cities. The cities will not be able to provide public services because there will be too many people living there. There will be more and more poor people."

**c** "OK, he said that his country has a scarcity of resources, especially water. That means there aren't enough resources. He said that the problem is partly because the population is getting bigger."

**B** 🔊 5.06 **IN PAIRS Listen to the first part of the presentation. Identify the main idea of what the man is saying and discuss how to express the same idea in your own words.**

**C** Look back at the words and phrases in bold in quotes 1–3 in **A**. Underline the adaptations Speaker 2 uses in quotes a–c.

**D** 🔊 5.07 **IN PAIRS Read and listen to the last part of the presentation. Then discuss how to adapt and simplify the language for someone who speaks less English than you do.**

There is no quick solution to all of these problems, but I'm convinced that one of the most pressing needs is water infrastructure, especially in rural areas. The government has the responsibility to encourage foreign investment in water infrastructure projects. We have a need for rainwater collection systems, irrigation systems, and water purification systems so that people will not have to leave the rural areas and move to the cities. With better water infrastructure, there would be increased employment opportunities in agriculture, and the country would have a greater supply of food.

**E** Discuss the questions as a class.

**1** Was it easy or difficult to simplify what the speaker said? Did you include explanations of certain words or phrases?

**2** Sometimes paraphrasing is a useful study tool even if you don't have to explain a written or spoken text to someone else. How can paraphrasing a text to yourself be useful?

## VOCABULARY review

SCORE: / 10

**A** Complete the text with the words and phrases from the box.

> admittedly    be upgraded    finding a cure for    frankly    given up on
> has an obligation to    have a chance to    have the ability to    landing on    make an attempt to

Here are my thoughts on the future of humanity. A lot of people have
**1** _____ the idea of making the world a better place.
They don't even **2** _____ do anything to help.
**3** _____, I think they would rather sit around and criticize
everything because that's easier than **4** _____ cancer or
**5** _____ Mars, isn't it? **6** _____,
there are a lot of problems in the world, but our generation **7** _____
do our best to solve the problems. One of the biggest problems is that our
technology infrastructure needs to **8** _____, but we
**9** _____ do that and so many other things. We
**10** _____ change the world, so come on, people;
let's get to work!

## GRAMMAR review

SCORE: / 10

**A** There are two errors in each sentence. Cross out the errors and write the correct forms.

**1** For the end of this semester, I will have be studying English for five years. _____,
_____

**2** My best friend will has arrived by the time tomorrow. _____, _____

**3** By the end of the year, how long you will have live here? _____, _____

**4** I will have been knowing my best friend in 10 years by the end of next month.
_____, _____

**5** I'm worried that I won't have been finishing my speech on tomorrow morning.
_____, _____

> **16–20 correct:** You can use adverbs of attitude, verb + noun + infinitive, and the language
> of progress.
> You can use future perfect and future perfect progressive.
> **0–15 correct:** Look again at the Vocabulary and Grammar sections in the unit.

TOTAL SCORE: / 20

### EXAM SKILLS  WRITING write an opinion essay

In one minute, think of three reasons why you agree or
disagree with this statement and write them below.

**There is no point in worrying about the future as we will not be here to experience it.**

_____

_____

_____

Go to Exams Skills on page 136–137 to learn how to prepare to write an opinion essay.

## Have a two-way discussion

In some exams, you have to hold a discussion with a partner or the person giving the test. In the discussion, you may need to answer questions or describe a picture.

**TACTIC 1:** Initiate the discussion and elicit responses.

**A** Put the words in order to form phrases and sentences. Then label the phrases and sentences for initiating a discussion (*I*) and for eliciting responses (*E*).

1  we / this / start / one / should / with / ? _____
   *Should we start ~~start one with~~ with this one?*

2  about / you / what / think / do / ... / ? _____
   *What do you think about?*

3  next / let's / point / about / talk / the / . _____
   _____

4  else / you / anything / can / think / of / ? _____ *Can*

5  other / do / ideas / have / any / you / ? _____
   *Do you have any other ideas*

6  on / to / we / move / should / the next point? _____
   *Should we move on the next*

7  talking / we / by / could / about / start / ... _____
   *We could start by talking more about*

8  say / anything / have / do / to / you / else / ? _____
   _____

**B** 🔊 **EXAM 1.01** Look at the mind map below. Listen to two speakers discussing the questions and prompts. Which phrases and sentences from **A** do they use in their discussion?

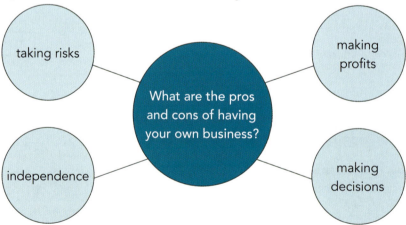

- taking risks
- making profits
- **What are the pros and cons of having your own business?**
- independence
- making decisions

**C** 🔊 **EXAM 1.01** Listen again. Complete the phrases and sentences the speakers use to ask for opinions and show agreement or disagreement.

1  Yes, that's ___definitely___ a pro.
2  I see ___your point___ but I also ___think___ it would be challenging.
3  Would ___you agree___ with that?
4  Yes, ___you're right___.
5  I ___completely___ agree with you.
6  It ___really___ depends.
7  ___I agree___ that it depends.

TACTIC 2: **Extend your responses.**

**A** Write the ideas from the box under the correct question in the table.

> easier to travel internationally
> less spending on storage and movement
> prevents healthy competition
>
> fewer small business opportunities
> lower rates of crime and fraud
> reduced spending in local economy

| What are the benefits of a society without cash? | What are the disadvantages of multinational companies? |
|---|---|
| _____ | _____ |
| _____ | _____ |
| _____ | _____ |

**B**  **EXAM 1.02** Listen to a speaker respond to a question about a society without cash. Complete the text with the transition phrases from the box.

> first of all, I would say that          for example
> finally, it's important to note that     I would also add that      this is because

That's an interesting question. **1** _____ *first for all* _____ in a society without cash, it would be easier to travel internationally. **2** _____ *Because* _____ there would be no need to change currency, and you could just use your credit card or phone to pay. **3** _____ banks and businesses would save money as they wouldn't have to pay for safe storage or movement of cash. **4** _____ *finally,* _____ there would probably be less crime and fraud. **5** _____ *for exam* _____, criminals would not be able to move money very easily in a cashless society as there would be a digital record of everything.

*100* **MAKE IT COUNT**

Remember to engage with your partner or the person giving the test and to use transitions to connect your ideas.

## EXAM PRACTICE

**A** Look at the mind map of the topics that people should think about before starting their own business. With your partner, discuss each of the topics and decide which to focus on.

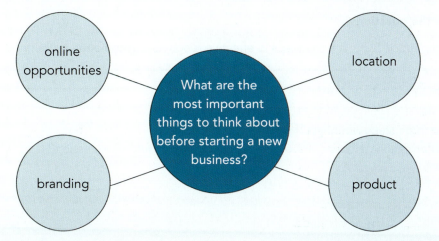

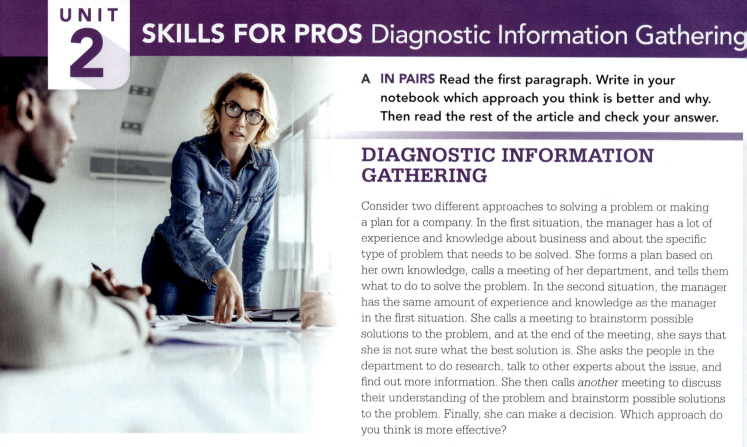

**A  IN PAIRS** Read the first paragraph. Write in your notebook which approach you think is better and why. Then read the rest of the article and check your answer.

## DIAGNOSTIC INFORMATION GATHERING

Consider two different approaches to solving a problem or making a plan for a company. In the first situation, the manager has a lot of experience and knowledge about business and about the specific type of problem that needs to be solved. She forms a plan based on her own knowledge, calls a meeting of her department, and tells them what to do to solve the problem. In the second situation, the manager has the same amount of experience and knowledge as the manager in the first situation. She calls a meeting to brainstorm possible solutions to the problem, and at the end of the meeting, she says that she is not sure what the best solution is. She asks the people in the department to do research, talk to other experts about the issue, and find out more information. She then calls *another* meeting to discuss their understanding of the problem and brainstorm possible solutions to the problem. Finally, she can make a decision. Which approach do you think is more effective?

You may think that the manager in the second situation is not a strong leader or that she doesn't know enough to solve the problem. However, if you believe that the saying "Two heads are better than one" is usually true, you may choose the second manager's approach. There are almost always different ways to think about and solve a problem, and it's generally better to have as much information as possible before making a final decision.

Diagnostic information gathering involves a number of things. First, you have to understand what kinds of information you need to solve a specific problem. Second, you should check with several different sources to make sure your information is as complete and correct as possible. Third, you should ask follow-up questions to make sure you get all the information you need or to clarify information.

Managers have to know how to get good information themselves, and they also have to make sure their employees have the information they need in order to make good decisions. This means that managers have to be able to interpret the information they receive, draw conclusions from it, and communicate the conclusions clearly to their employees.

Diagnostic information gathering skills are important in all types of professions, but one field where these skills are literally a matter of life or death is medicine. Doctors spend a lot of time attending conferences and reading journals in order to keep up with new information. To make correct diagnoses, they ask their patients many questions to make sure that the patients are giving complete and accurate information. Doctors frequently order medical tests to help them confirm or change a diagnosis, and they may consult other doctors to get their opinions. Some other professionals who use diagnostic information gathering every day are technicians who work on computers, phones, or other tech devices; meteorologists who create weather forecasts; and mechanics who repair cars and other vehicles. Think of how many mistakes could happen if people in very different types of work did not have good diagnostic information gathering skills and depended only on their own knowledge!

**B  IN PAIRS** Discuss the questions.

1   According to the article, what are the steps in effective diagnostic information gathering?
    Step 1: _____
    Step 2: _____
    Step 3: _____

2   Which of these three steps would you find the most difficult?

3   Is diagnostic information gathering important in your current or future profession? If so, why?

**C** **IN GROUPS** Read about the situation. Then answer and discuss the questions.

A group of students want to make the area around their school more attractive. They decided to design and create flower gardens and plant some trees, and the school director has given them permission to do the project. A couple of the students have some experience with gardening at home, but most of them have never worked in a garden. The group chooses one student with gardening experience to be the group leader, and she calls a meeting.

In the meeting, the group brainstorms all of the things they will need to consider while working on this project, but the group leader feels that there may be other important things to think about that the group is not aware of. She asks the group to research everything that they might need to consider when creating flower gardens and planting trees. She prepares a list of questions for them to answer.

1 What questions do you think the group leader might have asked?

_____

_____

2 How can the group do the research they need?

_____

_____

3 How should the group leader collect the information from the group?

_____

_____

4 What else should the group leader do during the project to make sure that it is successful?

_____

_____

**D** Discuss the questions.

1 In what other fields is diagnostic information gathering important? How is it used?
2 Read the first paragraph of the article again. What are the advantages of the first manager's approach?
3 What are the disadvantages of that approach?

**VIDEO**   **WATCH THE VIDEO AND LEARN ABOUT DIAGNOSTIC INFORMATION GATHERING**

**E** **IN GROUPS** Answer the questions.

1 What is the definition of "diagnostic information gathering"?
2 Where can you gather information?
3 Why is this skill important in an organization?
4 Which professions use diagnostic information gathering and why do they use this skill?
5 What examples of diagnostic information gathering could someone demonstrate for an interview?
6 What can you do to be a better researcher?

## Scan a test for easier questions

Before you start answering questions on a reading test, quickly look through them to decide which ones are easier to answer and do these ones first.

> **TACTIC 1:** Decide which questions are easier to answer and address them first. This will give you more time to answer the difficult ones.

**A** What kind of information are these questions asking about? Label questions 1–3 *M* (main ideas), *S* (specific details), or *O* (the writer's opinions or feelings). Which type of question do you think is easiest to answer? Why?

**1** What point does the writer make in the first paragraph? _____
 **a** Too much media attention is given to health.
 **b** Health will always be an important topic.

**2** How did the writer feel when he was in hospital? _____
 **a** relieved at the expertise of the medical staff
 **b** worried about paying an expensive bill

**3** According to paragraph 3, the number of doctors in the country in the last 20 years … _____
 **a** has increased steadily.
 **b** has stayed the same.

**B** Look at the questions in A again. Choose *True* or *False*.

| | | |
|---|---|---|
| **1** | Question 1 tells you exactly where to look in the text. | True / False |
| **2** | The options in question 1 are about different topics. | True / False |
| **3** | The options in question 2 have adjectives describing feeling. | True / False |
| **4** | In question 2, the reason for the writer's feeling in each option is the same. | True / False |
| **5** | In question 3, there are two specific pieces of information to guide you. | True / False |
| **6** | The options in question 3 are about a change in numbers. | True / False |

> **TACTIC 2:** Choose key words in questions about a reading to understand what you need to look for.

**A** Look at questions 1–3 from TACTIC 1 **A** and underline the key words or phrases.

 **MAKE IT COUNT**

Remember that you will not always see the same words in the questions as in the reading text. Look for synonyms and paraphrases.

**B** Decide which questions from TACTIC 1 **A** you want to answer first. Then read the text and underline the answers to the questions from TACTIC 1 **A** that you chose.

We hear a great deal about the health sector on a daily basis, whether it's on TV, on the radio, or on the news. People tend to pay attention to this information, whether they are in good health or not, and they generally believe that politicians are not doing enough to make access to facilities easier for everybody. Whether you agree with this or not, it's impossible to ignore the fact that there have always been people in society who need proper medical care. Regardless of how much money is spent on new hospitals, the topic will continue to be relevant.

I recently had firsthand experience of the health sector myself. An unfortunate accident on my bicycle meant I had to have some minor surgery, which involved a very brief stay in my local hospital. Before this, I had never really thought about the key role doctors and nurses play in our society. While my injuries were minor, I was comforted by just how capable they were in dealing

with not just me, but with other more serious medical problems around me. It's good to know that at least some of the money I pay in taxes goes toward supporting these professionals. While costly taxes can be a source of anxiety for many, they're there for a reason.

After my hospital experience, I decided to do some research into some general statistics on the state of our health service. With a growing population and with people living longer, there is an ever-increasing demand for hospital beds and medical professionals, particularly doctors. It's therefore surprising that the number of physicians has not really changed over the last two decades, meaning that there are fewer of them to deal with a growing number of patients. We cannot afford to ignore the need to recruit medical staff who are needed to take care of our population.

 **MAKE IT COUNT**

When you have identified which paragraph or paragraphs of the text will contain the answer, read that part in its entirety to make sure you understand it clearly.

# EXAM PRACTICE

**A** Read the questions. Write *M* next to the question on main ideas, *S* next to the question on specific details, and *O* next to the question on the writer's opinion. Decide in which order you will answer the questions.

**1** What are the benefits of medical students playing games like Wii? _____
   **a** They help trainee surgeons to relax.
   **b** They improve the skills needed to perform surgery.

**2** What is the value of medical students using a 3D simulator? _____
   **a** It can teach skills that are not formally taught.
   **b** It enables trainees to perform on live patients.

**3** What does the writer think about technology and learning? _____
   **a** Nowadays, most students prefer this format.
   **b** It makes learning fun and can be accessed anywhere.

**B** Read the text about video games and answer the questions from **A**.

Video games are increasingly being used as tools in medical education. In one study, a group of trainee surgeons were encouraged to play Wii games, like tennis and battle games, the idea being that if they play every day for an hour, within a month they should see an improvement in their hand-eye coordination. Significantly, the skills needed to control on-screen video game action are similar to those needed for keyhole surgery.

Another important skill for surgeons is clinical decision making; however, it often is not taught formally. Surgical simulators with 3D animations can help improve decision-making and problem-solving skills. In addition, studying anatomy in a three-dimensional space can really enhance the learning from textbooks and lectures. Such activities can also help users recognize risks—which nerves and arteries to avoid—without involving real human beings. At the same time, playing games makes learning come alive.

Although researchers say that more study is needed, there is growing evidence to show that games can be effective teaching tools in some circumstances. Students nowadays are used to accessing information through different devices and interacting with it. Today's technology can be accessed anytime and anywhere, and educational games make learning fun. If students can play while they learn the serious business of being a surgeon, that has to be a good thing.

# SKILLS FOR PROS Global Perspective

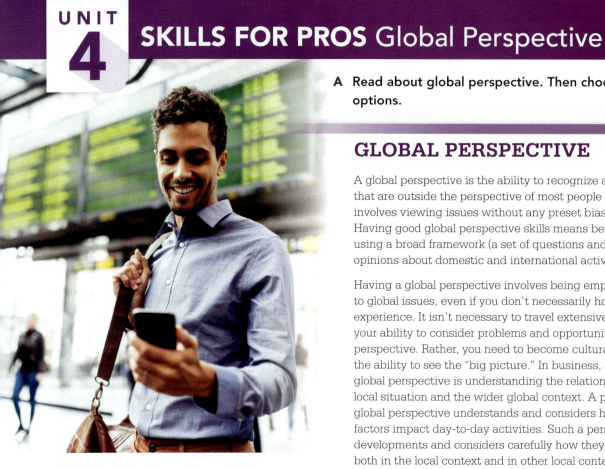

**A** Read about global perspective. Then choose the correct options.

## GLOBAL PERSPECTIVE

A global perspective is the ability to recognize and address issues that are outside the perspective of most people in your country. It involves viewing issues without any preset biases or limitations. Having good global perspective skills means being objective and using a broad framework (a set of questions and guidelines) to form opinions about domestic and international activities.

Having a global perspective involves being empathetic and sensitive to global issues, even if you don't necessarily have international experience. It isn't necessary to travel extensively to develop your ability to consider problems and opportunities from a global perspective. Rather, you need to become culturally aware and develop the ability to see the "big picture." In business, a key part of this global perspective is understanding the relationship between your local situation and the wider global context. A person with a good global perspective understands and considers how global and local factors impact day-to-day activities. Such a person is aware of global developments and considers carefully how they may affect business both in the local context and in other local contexts around the world.

In a multinational corporation, global perspective skills mean understanding the global strategy of the business and at the same time knowing how it influences local activities. For those in management positions, having a good global perspective means managing local interests while thinking about global considerations. It's also necessary to be proactive and plan ahead by preparing locally to support global activities. A manager with these skills acts as a role model for staff on global initiatives.

Having a global perspective is important in many different contexts. A salesperson working in the shipping industry, for example, needs to be aware of how global events may affect key international factors, such as changes in oil prices. The salesperson also needs to know how local considerations, such as environmental regulations, relate to global factors and may possibly affect demand for products and services. In addition, a police officer may be involved in an investigation that crosses international borders. In that case, it is important to demonstrate awareness of the laws local to all the countries affected by the case as well as any potential cultural differences. In marketing, an employee who is responsible for promoting a company in a number of different regions of the world is expected to match the global strategy to local expectations and culture.

Having a global perspective is vital for all employees. This is especially true as the world becomes increasingly connected and the relationship between local activities and global conditions becomes more important.

**1** A person with good global perspective skills …
   **a** spends time worrying about global problems.
   **b** considers problems without set ideas or prejudices.
   **c** knows that local problems are not particularly important.

**2** To develop your global perspective, you should …
   **a** try to understand other people's cultures.
   **b** make sure other people understand your culture.
   **c** go to as many other countries as possible.

**3** When you work for a large company, having a global perspective involves …
   **a** making your local area as productive as possible.
   **b** communicating your local needs to your managers.
   **c** knowing what the company wants to achieve globally and locally.

**4** In any profession, an employee with a global perspective needs to …
   **a** understand how people think and work in different countries.
   **b** know laws of their own country very well.
   **c** know how international events affect oil prices.

**B IN PAIRS** Discuss the questions.

**1** To what extent do you think you have a global perspective? Explain.

**2** How can you develop a global perspective if you do not have the opportunity to travel internationally?

**C IN GROUPS** Read the conversation. Discuss whether the company has a good global perspective and think of three suggestions of things they could do to improve.

Graham: Does anyone have the report on the release for our new satellite navigation app?

Gabriella: Sure, but it isn't good news. Sales in Asia are much lower than expected.

Graham: Really? Does the report have any explanation as to why that is happening?

Marco: Apparently, it is the controls on the interface. Users reported finding them hard to use while they are driving.

Graham: But we tested those controls with five different test groups. We have been testing this for over a year!

Marco: OK, but all the test groups were here in the US.

Gabriella: Right. Of course.

Graham: What? I don't see what difference that makes. Why does it matter the tests were done here?

Gabriella: Well, the report says that the app sells well in some Asian countries, but it is really unpopular in Japan, Thailand, Singapore, and Indonesia.

Graham: Right. So?

Marco: So all of those countries drive on the left but the app was only tested in the US by drivers who were driving on the right.

Graham: Oh. Right. That is bad news. The boss is not going to be happy.

**Suggestions**

1 _____

2 _____

3 _____

**D** Discuss the questions.

**1** In what ways is having a global perspective important in your career or desired career?

**2** Do you expect that having a global perspective will become more important as your career progresses?

**3** How can you improve your understanding of global perspective skills?

## VIDEO  WATCH THE VIDEO AND LEARN ABOUT GLOBAL PERSPECTIVE

**E IN GROUPS** Answer the questions.

**1** Why is it important to have "global perspective" as a job skill?

**2** Why is this skill important in today's economy?

**3** How can you demonstrate global perspective in an interview?

**4** What impact does global perspective have on the social side of your career?

**5** What can you do to develop a global perspective?

**6** What is the benefit of having a global perspective and getting to know other cultures?

## Write an opinion essay

In an opinion essay task, you should use semiformal or formal language and give reasons to support your opinion.

> **TACTIC 1:** Write your main idea and opinion in the introductory paragraph. Write about one reason in each body paragraph. Sum up your ideas in the concluding paragraph.

**A**  Read the essay prompt. Circle the ideas in the box that are appropriate to include in the essay.

> Prompt: Many people think that technology will continue to change our lives for the better. Do you agree or disagree?

| | |
|---|---|
| cost of buying a smartphone | development of artificial intelligence |
| effect of technology on learning | history of the first computer |
| impact of social media on relationships | use of email and text messages |

**B**  Read the essay in response to the prompt in **A**. Match the paragraphs with their topics.

**1**  Technology will certainly continue to impact our lives in several ways. In this essay, I will argue that while it can change our lives for the better, there can also be some drawbacks.

**2**  On one hand, there are huge benefits from developing technology. Take education and learning, for example. It is increasingly possible for people to study online and to participate in courses that they would otherwise not be able to. Technology in the classroom also makes learning more fun and interesting for students, and the fact that less paper is being used is obviously an advantage for the environment.

**3**  Artificial intelligence, too, will continue to get better. This benefits us in many ways. For instance, many people have robotic vacuum cleaners that can clean their floors or smart fridges that notify you when you do not have certain items. Having said that, however, increased artificial intelligence poses a threat to many jobs e.g., self-checkout machines in supermarkets. If technology is able to learn and do more and more tasks, then more and more people will be out of a job.

**4**  If we look at the impact of technology on our relationships, particularly in terms of social media, it is hard to see how this will continue to make our lives better. People are becoming increasingly absorbed by their social media accounts. This causes usual human interactions and pastimes like participating in sports or joining clubs to suffer. It is important to remember that we can also interact with real people on a daily basis.

**5**  To conclude, it is clear that technology will continue to develop and impact our lives in positive ways, but there are also drawbacks we should be aware of.

Paragraph 1 (Introduction) _____
Paragraph 2 (Body Paragraph) _____
Paragraph 3 (Body Paragraph) _____
Paragraph 4 (Body Paragraph) _____
Paragraph 5 (Conclusion) _____

**a**  effect of technology on learning
**b**  writer's opinion about technology's effects
**c**  effects of social media on relationships
**d**  writer's conclusion about technology's effects
**e**  effects of technology on artificial intelligence

> **TACTIC 2:** Support your opinion with reasons and examples. Use one paragraph for each reason that supports your opinion. Include two or three examples to support each reason. Keep a list of useful phrases to introduce reasons and examples.

**A** Look at the essay again. Write the supporting examples the writer uses in each body paragraph.

**1** Paragraph 2

a _____

b _____

c _____

**2** Paragraph 3

a _____

b _____

**3** Paragraph 4

a _____

b _____

**B** Read the essay again. Write the phrase the writer uses to introduce each idea. What phrases does the writer use in each paragraph to organize their thoughts and ideas? What are the phrases used for?

| | |
|---|---|
| Paragraph 1 | |
| Paragraph 2 | |
| Paragraph 3 | |
| Paragraph 4 | |
| Paragraph 5 | |

 **MAKE IT COUNT**

For an opinion essay, there is no right or wrong answer. The most important thing is to be able to support your point of view with reasons and examples.

## EXAM PRACTICE

**A** In your English class, you have been talking about the consequences of a growing population on the planet. Your teacher has asked you to write an essay for homework. Write your essay in 250–300 words.

> If the global population continues to grow, there will be serious consequences for the planet. Do you agree or disagree?

# SPEAKING PRACTICE

## Unit 1, p. 12

### ASK ABOUT IT

- What products is your country famous for around the world?
- How international are the foods in your house?
- What are the traditional foods in your area of the country?

### TALK ABOUT IT

- Mexico is famous for tacos, but there are also many cultural products such as TV programs and …
- In my house, we typically eat food from this country, but when we go out to a restaurant …
- Where I'm from, we eat choripán, which is a kind of sandwich. We also eat …

## Unit 1, p. 15

### ASK ABOUT IT

- Does your family buy more things from local businesses or global businesses?
- What are the benefits of having the same businesses around the world?
- How do local businesses help the local economy?

### TALK ABOUT IT

- My family likes to buy from big shops that have everything, but sometimes when we need …
- Global businesses help to maintain a high standard of product. Another benefit is that …
- The money from local businesses normally goes to local places like markets. Also, customers need to go to the center of town, which means …

## Unit 2, p. 24

### ASK ABOUT IT

- Why is it important for sports to keep changing?
- Which improvements to sports have made them more dangerous?
- If you could make any improvement to any sport, what would it be?

### TALK ABOUT IT

- People prefer faster sports with high scores, so sports need to change in order to …
- The safety equipment in some sports offers a lot of protection, but it also means that athletes believe that …
- I would like to see sports in the air. We have sports in water, and many on the ground but …

## Unit 2, p. 27

### ASK ABOUT IT

- Where does the money for sports come from in your country?
- Which sports do you think deserve more promotion and more funding?
- Are there any groups in your country who need more support to get involved in sports?

### TALK ABOUT IT

- Most of the money for sports comes from private companies. The problem with that is …
- Frescobol is a sport played on the beach here in Brazil, but internationally, it isn't really …
- Often the female versions of sports are not shown on TV, or if they are, they do not …

## Unit 3, p. 36

### ASK ABOUT IT

- Do your family and friends use private health care or public health care more? Why?
- How have medical services improved in your country?
- How would your life be different now if medical services hadn't improved in your country?

### TALK ABOUT IT

- Public health care is good in my country, but you have to wait a long time so my family …
- The technology that doctors use has improved a lot in recent years. However, not all doctors …
- I'm sure my grandparents would not be as healthy as they are now if doctors hadn't started using …

## Unit 3, p. 39

### ASK ABOUT IT

- What areas of medicine would benefit from using robots?
- How could technology improve people's health in the future?
- How should society limit the use of technology in medicine?

### TALK ABOUT IT

- I think robots are good for physically difficult tasks like lifting patients, but they aren't good at tasks that need social interaction like …
- I think that nanotechnology is one area that will really change the future of health care because …
- Technology will definitely help to improve people's health, but there are some ethical considerations like …

## Unit 4, p. 48

### ASK ABOUT IT

- Should cities be planned around natural features or designed for human use?
- What do you like about the design of your favorite city/cities?
- How would you change the design of your city?

### TALK ABOUT IT

- I think that we should respect the natural features of the place you live, but to make a city suitable for people to live in, you need to …
- My city has a lot of green spaces such as parks, which makes it very attractive. It also has …
- The traffic in my city is terrible, so we need to do something that will improve …

## Unit 4, p. 51

### ASK ABOUT IT

- Why is it important for countries to create sustainable buildings?
- How could governments help to encourage the creation of sustainable buildings?
- What are the most common features of sustainable architecture in your area?

### TALK ABOUT IT

- Sustainable buildings cause fewer problems for the environment, so it is important …
- To help families make their homes sustainable, governments could offer families money or …
- It is common to see solar panels where I live, and also, in some places, you can see …

## Unit 5, p. 60

### ASK ABOUT IT

- Which areas of society will change the most in the next hundred years?
- Which areas of society will be the hardest to change?
- Which changes do you think you will see in your lifetime?

### TALK ABOUT IT

- Transportation will change dramatically because of new environmentally friendly technology …
- The hardest thing to change will be how houses are built because people do not change houses often …
- In my lifetime, I think people will explore new planets and discover new …

## Unit 5, p. 63

### ASK ABOUT IT

- How will society get the resources it needs?
- What is the best way to find imaginative solutions to the problems we face?
- Which problems will be the easiest to solve?

### TALK ABOUT IT

- In my opinion, we need to start looking in places that we haven't looked already: the ocean, other planets …
- I think we need to get the opinions of people with different perspectives instead of always …
- The easiest problems to solve will be the ones that affect the most people because many people will …

# Irregular Verbs

| Infinitive | Simple past | Past participle |
|---|---|---|
| be | was/were | been |
| become | became | become |
| begin | began | begun |
| break | broke | broken |
| bring | brought | brought |
| build | built | built |
| buy | bought | bought |
| catch | caught | caught |
| choose | chose | chosen |
| come | came | come |
| cost | cost | cost |
| cut | cut | cut |
| do | did | done |
| draw | drew | drawn |
| drink | drank | drunk |
| drive | drove | driven |
| eat | ate | eaten |
| fall | fell | fallen |
| feed | fed | fed |
| feel | felt | felt |
| find | found | found |
| fly | flew | flown |
| get | got | gotten |
| give | gave | given |
| go | went | gone |
| grow | grew | grown |
| hang | hung | hung |
| have | had | had |
| hear | heard | heard |
| hit | hit | hit |
| hold | held | held |
| hurt | hurt | hurt |
| keep | kept | kept |
| know | knew | known |
| leave | left | left |
| let | let | let |
| lose | lost | lost |
| make | made | made |
| meet | met | met |
| pay | paid | paid |
| put | put | put |
| read | read | read |
| ride | rode | ridden |
| ring | rang | rung |
| rise | rose | risen |
| run | ran | run |
| say | said | said |
| see | saw | seen |
| sell | sold | sold |
| send | sent | sent |
| set | set | set |
| sing | sang | sung |
| sit | sat | sat |
| speak | spoke | spoken |
| stand | stood | stood |
| stick | stuck | stuck |
| take | took | taken |
| teach | taught | taught |
| tell | told | told |
| think | thought | thought |
| throw | threw | thrown |
| understand | understood | understood |
| wake | woke | woken |
| wear | wore | worn |
| win | won | won |
| write | wrote | written |

# Pronunciation Symbols

## Vowels

| | |
|---|---|
| ɪ | did |
| ɛ | bed |
| æ | bad |
| ʌ | cup |
| ʊ | book |
| ə | banana |
| i | feed |
| ɑ | father, box |
| ɔ | tall |
| u | student, food |
| ɚ | shirt, birthday |
| eɪ | date, table |
| aɪ | cry, eye |
| ɔɪ | boy |
| oʊ | comb, post |
| aʊ | about, how |

## Consonants

| | |
|---|---|
| p | park, happy |
| b | back, hobby |
| t | tea |
| d | die |
| k | came, kitchen, quarter |
| g | game, go |
| f | face, photographer |
| V | vegetable |
| θ | thing, math |
| ð | then, that |
| s | city, summer |
| z | please, goes |
| ʃ | she, shop |
| ʒ | leisure |
| h | hot, who |
| tʃ | chicken, watch |
| dʒ | jacket, orange |
| m | men |
| n | sun, know |
| ŋ | sung, singer |
| w | week, white |
| r | rain, writer |
| l | light, long |
| j | yes, use, music |

**A** Complete the paragraphs with the infinitive or gerund form of the verb in parentheses.

It's been a big adjustment moving to the United States to study. The university system is very different from the system at home. For one thing, the school permits us **1** _____ (choose) our majors in our second or third year instead of **2** _____ (choose) one right away. Also, classes consist of lectures, discussions, and projects—not just lectures. A lecturer will even stop **3** _____ (answer) a question in the middle of a talk. We are expected to ask questions, and I'm not used to **4** _____ (do) that.

One good thing is the students are really friendly. I live in a dorm, and my roommate and I have become good friends. She recently invited me **5** _____ (visit) her parents. I have to remember **6** _____ (bring) a gift, but I'm not sure what to get. In addition to **7**_____ (go) to class, lots of students belong to clubs. On the weekends, everyone seems to go to parties and sporting events, such as football games. Not me. That's when I end up **8** _____ (do) most of my studying.

**B** Choose the correct option.

1 You **are allowed to wear** / **are required to wear** long sleeves at work. It's a new rule.
2 My boss often **makes me stay** / **lets me stay** late on Fridays. It's pretty annoying.
3 We **can't take** / **are encouraged to take** an hour for lunch. If we do, we'll get in trouble.
4 She **is required to complete** / **doesn't have to complete** her expense reports. Her assistant does them for her.
5 If you don't understand something, you **have to ask** / **should ask** questions. It's not a problem.
6 Please **let me help** / **must I help** you with those heavy bags. I can carry some for you.
7 It's fine to have food at your desk, but you **aren't required to have** / **shouldn't have** drinks.
8 **Should I leave** / **Can I leave** a few minutes early tomorrow, please?

**C** Unscramble the words to make sentences.

1 get help / I / unless / can't finish / I / the design
   I _____.
2 her job / February / has / she / at / since / worked
   She _____.
3 expensive / for more / they / if the project / will look / funding / is too
   They _____.
4 in case / sell out / they / soon / bought tickets / I / early
   I _____.
5 provided that / working / will take / it's / they / the elevator
   They _____.
6 will go up / it's / to the observation deck / we / as long as / free
   We _____.

**D** Rewrite the sentences as reported speech. Use the verb in parentheses to report the information.

1 Jennifer has been home sick all day. (explained)
   She _____.
2 Frank criticizes Jasmin's fashion choices. (mentioned)
   He _____.
3 Ursula was a model in her teens. (told me)
   She _____.
4 Lily will go to fashion school. (predicted)
   He _____.
5 Patrice may take a semester off to travel. (said)
   She _____.
6 Emilio should consider a career in design. (stated)
   He _____.

**E** Complete the paragraph with the correct words from the box.

| | |
|---|---|
| **a** do | **e** who funded the movie |
| **b** bigger | **f** which include both domestic and international sales |
| **c** more | **g** that does poorly at home |
| **d** more and more | **h** which is another name for a complete failure |

Have you seen the movie *The 13th Warrior*? No? Not many people did. The 1999 movie made $60 million around the world. While that sounds like a lot, it cost $160 million to make the movie. It lost $100 million. In other words, it was a flop, **1** _____. Movie flops can be big or small. The **2** _____ money lost, the **3** _____ the flop. To figure out if a movie is a flop, you need to look at overall ticket sales, **4** _____. If the movie brings in more money than it costs to make, it's considered a success. For example, an American movie **5** _____ may make a lot of money overseas. But sometimes movies that initially seem to be flops **6** _____ make money over time. The producers **7** _____ might later make money by selling movie rights so that it can be shown on TV or through streaming services. But generally, producers don't like to take risks, and they are becoming **8** _____ cautious when it comes to funding big-budget movies.

**F** Choose the correct option.

**1** I will rather travel / **would rather travel** by plane than by boat.
**2** I am sure that soon more environmentally friendly fabrics **will be used** / will be using for clothing.
**3** I was calling / **was going to call** you last night, but I decided not to.
**4** I felt anxious all morning. I **was giving** / will be given a presentation later that day.
**5** **I will be sitting** / will prefer to sit on a beach at this time tomorrow.
**6** When the plane finally landed, we were waiting / **had been waiting** for over 90 minutes.
**7** Miguel had learned / **had been learning** four languages by the time he was in high school.
**8** I will prefer / **would prefer** to go out for dinner tonight.

**G** Find and correct one error in each sentence. Rewrite the sentence correctly.

**1** There are only a little customers in the store. _____
**2** I bought a wooden beautiful bowl in Ecuador. _____
**3** I stopped to eat meat 15 years ago. _____
**4** What he has three jobs is remarkable. _____
**5** Can you put little sugar in my coffee, please? _____
**6** It was hard at first, but I'm used to eat with chopsticks now. _____

**H** Choose the correct option.

My friend Kal and I were traveling through Southeast Asia. Today, he started to hold his stomach. At first, I thought he **1 may have been** / couldn't have been hungry, but then I saw that he was in pain. I wondered if he **2 might have eaten** / mustn't have eaten something bad. But he **3 may have done** / couldn't have done that because we'd been eating the same thing every day. Then I realized what happened. He **4 must have drunk** / may not have drunk some bad water. Kal never buys water and just gets water from the tap. He sometimes boils it, but he **5 might have boiled** / must not have boiled it yesterday. He **6 could have bought** / must have bought water on several occasions, when I did, but he said he wanted to save his money for other things. I hope he feels better. And I hope he's learned his lesson!

# Grammar Reference

## UNIT 1—review of perfect forms

### Function

The perfect tenses are used to indicate a completed action. Perfect tenses generally put the focus on the present even though the action occurred in the past. For progressive tenses, the focus is on the duration of the action.

We use the **present perfect** for a situation that began in the past and is still true.

We use the **present perfect progressive** for an action that started in the past and continued until another event happened.

We use the **past perfect** to express a situation or an event that happened before another past situation or event.

We use the **past perfect progressive** for an action that continued until another event happened.

Remember that we can use stative verbs with simple perfect tenses, but not progressive perfect tenses. Stative verbs include verbs of possession (*own, consist, have*), senses (*hear, smell, sound*), emotion (*like, prefer, adore*), and mental states (*know, believe, doubt*).

### Form

| Present perfect simple | have + not + past participle | I **have gotten** high grades in my economics and finance classes. |
|---|---|---|
| Present perfect progressive | have + not + been + verb -ing | My financial advisor **has been trading** in Bitcoin for years. |
| Past perfect simple | had + not + past participle | I **hadn't heard** about their products before I started trading with them. |
| Past perfect progressive | had + not + been + verb -ing | The economy **had been growing** for a year before it collapsed. |

**A** Choose the correct option.

Leroy Bautista **1 has worked** / had been working in kitchens for 25 years before losing his job as a chef. He saw this as an opportunity. He decided to do what his friends **2 has told** / had been telling him to do – open a business selling his homemade sauces. The company Nic & Luc Jam was soon born. They **3 had sold** / have been selling jarred jams ever since.

And they're growing. Nic & Luc Jam **4 hadn't been** / haven't been selling many varieties of jam before they expanded. Nic & Luc Jam now sell 17 flavors. They use no artificial ingredients and only buy local produce. This **5 has made** / had been making them different from the competition.

Bautista **6 has known** / has been knowing for years that it is important to support other local businesses like his own. He **7 has said** / had been saying that profitability is important for any small business, but he **8 hasn't forgotten** / hadn't been forgetting about other small business owners in his community. He is known for giving back and helping others as needed.

## UNIT 1—articles

### Function

We use indefinite articles (*a*, *an*) before nouns to indicate the nouns are general. We use the definite article (*the*) before nouns to indicate they are specific. Sometimes we do not use any article at all.

### Form

| Use *a/an* … | |
| --- | --- |
| to talk about one of many things. | Let's stop at **a** food truck for lunch. |
| to talk about something for the first time. | I read **an** interesting book. It was about … |
| **Use *the* …** | |
| when it's clear what we're talking about, often because we've mentioned it before. | Why was **the** book interesting? |
| with superlative forms. | This is **the** largest expansion in our history. |
| for the names of rivers, seas, oceans, mountain ranges, deserts, plural country names, and island groups. | The Nile River flows into **the** Mediterranean Sea. |
| for the names of theaters, hotels, museums, and art galleries. | The Plaza Hotel and **the** Metropolitan Museum of Art are in New York City. |
| **Use no article …** | |
| with a plural noun. | We are investing in hotels and restaurants. |
| with uncountable nouns. | Education and training are important to us. |
| with the names of most countries, continents, states, mountains, and lakes. | Mount McKinley is in Alaska. |
| with the names of most towns, cities, neighborhoods, and streets. | Soho is a neighborhood in New York City. |

**A  Write *the* or X (no article).**

1 _____ Beverly Hills Hotel
2 _____ Mississippi River
3 _____ South Africa
4 _____ Andes Mountains
5 _____ Canada

6 _____ Caribbean Sea
7 _____ Lake Titicaca
8 _____ Mount Everest
9 _____ United States
10 _____ Miami

11 _____ British Museum
12 _____ Second Avenue
13 _____ Galapagos islands
14 _____ Philippines
15 _____ Museum of Modern Art

**B  Look at these steps for starting a business. Write *a*, *an*, *the*, or X (no article).**

Step 1: Do your research. **1** _____ first thing you need to do is see if there's **2** _____ market for your product or service.

Step 2: Write **3** _____ business plan. It's **4** _____ essential document if you're looking for **5** _____ bank loan.

Step 3: Get **6** _____ legal advice. Attorneys help you manage the risks of being **7** _____ business owner.

Step 4: Choose **8** _____ great name for your business. Remember, **9** _____ best business names are unique, memorable, and easy to pronounce.

Step 5: Find out if you need to get **10** _____ tax ID number. Depending on where you live, most businesses are required to have one.

Step 6: Open **11** _____ business bank account. While you're doing that, get **12** _____ business credit card that offers reward points.

Step 7: Talk to **13** _____ accountant. Get advice on **14** _____ best tax filing status for your business.

Step 8: Get **15** _____ business license. Contact experts to find out what's required in your industry or use **16** _____ online resource.

## UNIT 2—verb + gerund

### Function

A gerund (verb + -ing) is used as a noun. It can go after a verb, such as *I like swimming*. It can also go after a verb + object, a verb + time expression, or a verb + expression of place.

### Form

| Use | Examples |
|---|---|
| Use a gerund after the verb *have* + object (*difficulty, fun, trouble, a good time, an easy time, a hard time*). | We **had fun doing** aerobics.<br>She **had a difficult time understanding** us. |
| Use a gerund after a verb of perception (*hear, listen, notice, observe, see, watch*) + object. | I **watched her playing** volleyball.<br>He **noticed me practicing** golf. |
| Use a gerund after the verb *spend* or *waste* + a time expression (*time, hours, a lot of time, two years, an eternity*). | He **spent two years playing** professional tennis.<br>I **wasted a lot of time playing** video games. |
| Use a gerund after the verbs *sit, stand,* or *lie* + an expression of place (*here, there, on the sofa, on the bed, at your desk, in your room*). | He's **lying on the bed reading** a magazine.<br>Why **are you sitting** at your desk eating lunch? |

A  **Choose the correct verbs. Then complete the sentences with the gerund form of the verb in parentheses.**

1  They had / saw trouble _____ (find) their seats at the stadium.
2  She had / spent a long time _____ (study) her opponent.
3  Why are you having / lying in bed _____ (watch) TV?
4  Did you listen / see those people _____ (sell) tickets to the sold-out game?
5  I noticed / wasted some people _____ (record) the game with their phones.
6  We are having / spending a hard time _____ (fund) our team.
7  He's sitting / having on the floor _____ (play) a game.
8  Please don't waste / hold your time _____ (read) comic books.

B  **Complete the information with the gerund form of the verbs from the box.**

> be   deal   encourage   observe   play   work

Kids have fun **1** _____ sports and they learn key life skills through them.
One is respect. Watching a coach **2** _____ team members to respect
each other shows that the human relationship in sports is important. Sports also teach kids
friendship. Kids form important bonds through sports, and this leads to lasting friendships.

Winning sports games is not easy, and everyone has a hard time **3** _____
with loss. But losing games helps kids learn to handle problems better. They become stronger
when they learn that wasting time **4** _____ upset over a loss is not helpful.
They learn to continue doing their best when they play sports.

Sports also help with leadership skills. Even if players spend most of their time just
**5** _____ a game instead of playing a game, they see what good
leadership involves.

And finally, kids learn about teamwork through sports. As they watch their teammates
**6** _____ together to achieve a common goal, they realize there is truth to
the saying "There is no 'I' in team."

# UNIT 2—relative pronouns with -ever; no matter

## Function

When we add -ever to the pronouns *what*, *which*, *when*, *where*, *who*, and *how*, the reference is not specific. It means any thing, place, time, person, or way.

**whatever**: anything at all; it doesn't matter what
**whichever**: any one at all; it doesn't matter which
**whenever**: any time at all; it doesn't matter when
**wherever**: any place at all; it doesn't matter where
**whoever**: any person at all; it doesn't matter who
**however**: any way at all; it doesn't matter how

The phrase *no matter* means something is true in all cases. For example:

*No matter who you talk to, you'll find they support sports in schools.* =

*Every person you talk to supports sports in schools.*

## Form

| pronoun + verb | **Whoever said** that the new player is not a good teammate hasn't seen him in many games. |
| --- | --- |
| pronoun + subject + verb | **Whatever you do**, don't insult our corporate sponsor.<br>There are crazy sports fans **wherever you go.** |
| pronoun + object + subject + verb | **Whichever date for the game you choose** is fine with me.<br>Do your best **whatever sport you** participate in. |
| *no matter* + pronoun + clause | I'll enjoy the game **no matter who wins** in the end. |

**A** **Match the parts to make sentences.**

1 Coaches are free to train their teams _____
2 I always try to watch _____
3 There are lots of sports clubs to choose from _____
4 I have extra tickets to the match, so feel free to invite _____
5 I'll be happy to go to either game, so I'm fine with _____
6 I can't understand the rules of American football _____
7 Please don't forget to bring our tickets to the game, _____

**a** whatever you do.
**b** whichever one you choose.
**c** wherever you live.
**d** however they like.
**e** whoever you like.
**f** no matter how you explain them.
**g** whenever my team is playing.

**B** **Choose the correct option.**

1 I will never understand the research **however** / **no matter** you try to explain it.
2 **Whatever** / **Whichever** you do, don't mention last Friday's game to Coach Nelson.
3 You can cheer the Red Shirts or the Blue Shirts. Choose **however** / **whichever** you like.
4 Report for practice **whenever** / **wherever** you get here.
5 Maggie will do what she wants **no matter** / **however** what you say.
6 James gets angry **no matter** / **whenever** the coach gives him constructive criticism.
7 Because it's your birthday, we can go **wherever** / **whoever** you like tonight.
8 **Whoever** / **Whatever** ordered those uniforms paid too much.

# UNIT 3—mixed conditionals

## Function

In a mixed conditional, the clauses in the sentence refer to different times. They are used to describe unreal situations. There are two types of mixed conditionals. One describes the present result of a past condition, and the other describes the past result of a present condition.

## Form

| Present result of a past condition | |
| --- | --- |
| The *if* clause is in the past perfect tense. The main clause uses *would* + base form of verb or *would* + *be* + verb-*ing*. | If Ken **had graduated** from college, he **would have** a good job now. (But he didn't graduate from college, so he doesn't have a good job now.)<br><br>If I **hadn't quit** medical school, I **would be working** as a doctor now. (But I did quit, so I am not a doctor.) |
| Past result of a present or continuing condition | |
| The *if* clause is in the simple past tense. The main clause uses *would have* + past participle. (Note: In the *if*-clause, always use *were* for the simple past tense of *be*.) | If Ming **weren't** busy every evening, he **would have come** to the party. (But Ming is busy every evening, so he didn't come.)<br><br>If she **knew** your schedule, she **would have invited** you over last weekend, (But she doesn't know your schedule, so she didn't invite you.) |

**A** Choose the correct option. Think about whether it is the present result of a past condition or the past result of present or continuing condition.

1 If he had worn sunblock, he **wouldn't be** / **wouldn't have been** sunburned now.
2 She **wouldn't make** / **wouldn't have made** her teacher peanut butter cookies if she knew about her teacher's peanut allergy.
3 We **would be** / **would have been** at the beach now if we had taken the train.
4 If I **am** / **were** less shy, I would have asked the doctor more questions.
5 If she **went** / **had gone** to nursing school, she would be working as a nurse now.
6 You wouldn't feel so sick if you **didn't eat** / **hadn't eaten** so much food.

**B** Complete these mixed conditionals with the correct form of the verbs in parentheses.

1 If I _____ (be) more ambitious, I _____ (study) to become a surgeon.
2 You _____ (get) the internship if your resume _____ (be) more impressive.
3 If I _____ (listen) to your advice, I _____ (not have) these problems now.
4 The doctor _____ (give) you that drug if you _____ (not have) an allergy to it.
5 You _____ (feel) fine now if you _____ (not work) for 24 hours without a break.
6 He _____ (not be) sick today if he _____ (take) his medicine as directed.
7 I _____ (apply) for the hospital job if I _____ (not be) afraid of the sight of blood.
8 If we _____ (not trust) him with our grandmother, we _____ (not ask) him to be her nurse.

# UNIT 3—clauses of contrast and purpose

## Function

We use clauses of purpose to show the use or purpose of something or why someone does something. We use clauses of contrast to compare two things or two situations. There are various ways to express either type of clause.

## Form

| Clauses of contrast | Examples |
| --- | --- |
| *despite / in spite of* + gerund | **Despite feeling** better, she spent an additional day in the hospital. |
| *despite / in spite of* + noun phrase | Many people have the flu **in spite of the increased number of flu vaccinations.** |
| *despite / in spite of the fact that* + clause | **Despite the fact that it was very expensive**, she had the surgery. |
| *though / although / even though* + subject + verb | **Although working as an emergency room nurse is challenging**, Rhonda enjoys her job. |
| **Clauses of purpose** | **Examples** |
| *for* + gerund | The MRI machine is used **for scanning** the brain. |
| *so as to / in order to* + base form | The doctor inserted the device **in order to monitor** the patient's heart. |
| *so that* + subject + modal verb | I went to the hospital nursery window **so that I could** see the newborn baby. |

**A  Complete these sentences with the words and phrases from the box.**

despite   for   in spite   so as to   so that   though

1   He stayed home from work _____ avoid spreading his cold.
2   The medicine helped get rid of the flu, _____ it took several days to do so.
3   The doctor gave me these pills _____ decreasing pain.
4   Some people still won't get flu vaccinations, _____ the evidence they help prevent the flu.
5   The doctor took X-rays of my leg _____ he could see if it was broken.
6   She continued to walk _____ of the pain it caused her.

**B  Circle the correct option.**

3D printers are used **1 so that  /  for** creating three-dimensional objects. Developers first used them **2 in order to  /  so that** duplicate everyday objects, but now "bioprinters" are being used to create living body parts. **3 In spite  /  Despite** some early ethical concerns, scientists are moving ahead with the process in order **4 for meeting  /  to meet** increasing demand. They use human cells as "ink" and the bioprinter layers cells **5 so as to  /  in spite of** make human tissues and organs. To create an ear, for example, the printer creates a soft scaffold made of hydrogel **6 in order to  /  so that** the cells have something to grow on. After six months, the hydrogel disintegrates, leaving an ear made of human cells. Scientists use the patient's cells, **7 although  /  so that** this isn't always possible. **8 In spite of  /  So that** previous success duplicating livers, bladders, and kidneys, scientists caution that 3D printing may not work for every body part. 3D printing of the brain, for example, may never be possible.

## UNIT 4—inverted conditionals

### Function

We can invert first, second, and third conditional sentences. In inverted conditionals, the word *if* is omitted and the word order is changed. We generally use inverted conditionals in more formal communication.

### Form

| *If* clause conditional | Inverted conditional |
|---|---|
| First: | |
| If you fly over Brasilia, you will see the grid pattern from the air. | Should you fly over Brasilia, you will see the grid pattern from the air. |
| If you care about city planning, you will want to come to the next city council meeting. | Should you care about city planning, you will want to come to the next city council meeting. |
| Second: | |
| If you studied urban planning, you would understand the challenges that planners face. | Were you to study urban planning, you would understand the challenges that planners face. |
| If it weren't for Mr. Diaz, there would still be deep holes in many of our roads. | Were it not for Mr. Diaz, there would still be deep holes in many of our roads. |
| Third: | |
| If you had been at the meeting, we would have had enough people to argue our case. | Had you been at the meeting, we would have had enough people to argue our case. |
| If the founders had planned for a larger city, we wouldn't have needed a new sewage system. | Had the founders planned for a larger city, we wouldn't have needed a new sewage system. |

**A** Rewrite each sentence into an inverted conditional sentence.

1 If more taxes went toward infrastructure, there wouldn't be a budget deficit.

   _____

2 If I get a chance to visit Washington, DC, I'll visit the Jefferson Memorial first.

   _____

3 If the pedestrians had known about the construction, they would have taken a different route.

   _____

4 If you build a luxury hotel in the city, it will bring in more visitors.

   _____

5 If it weren't for the petition, the city would not have new bus stops.

   _____

6 If you had called the city planning office, they would have told you what forms you need.

   _____

**B** Complete the inverted conditional sentences with the correct form of the verb in parentheses.

1 _____ we _____ (need) more funding for the project, we will have to revise our proposal.

2 Were we to choose just one architect, we _____ (choose) Ms. Hansen.

3 _____ she _____ (be) present, she would have spoken in favor of the proposal.

4 Were it not for Yvette, we _____ (not know) about this plan.

5 Should you need me, I _____ (be) in the library.

6 Had the residents not been so persistent, we _____ (not get) approval for the new playground in the park.

7 Were they to widen the tunnel, large trucks _____ (be) able to go through.

8 _____ the city workers _____ (not reach) an agreement, they will go on a strike.

# UNIT 4—review of adverbs

## Function

Adverbs are words that modify or qualify other types of words, such as adjectives, verbs, clauses, or other adverbs. There are different types of adverbs for describing how, where, when, in what manner, and for what purpose something is done or happens.

## Form

| Use | Examples |
|---|---|
| Use adverbs of manner to say how something is done. | quickly, gently, fast, perfectly, recklessly |
| Use adverbs of definite frequency to say when or how often something happens. | daily, weekly, annually, twice, finally |
| Use adverbs of indefinite frequency to say how often something is done. | often, usually, always, frequently, seldom |
| Use adverbs of purpose to say the reason something is done and join two clauses. | since, therefore, consequently, as a result, in order to |

**A  Look at the adverb types above and choose the correct adverb from the box.**

> already   because   constantly   eventually   firmly   hastily   sometimes   thus

1  The streets in this town _____ need to be repaired. (adverb of indefinite frequency)
2  The heating filters need to be replaced _____ they are too old. (adverb of purpose)
3  We have _____ approved the design of the new school. (adverb of definite frequency)
4  Stone is a strong building material. _____, it lasts a long time. (adverb of purpose)
5  Homeowners _____ put wooden fences around their homes. (adverb of indefinite frequency)
6  Some buildings are constructed _____ and have problems later. (adverb of manner)
7  After several years, they _____ realized they needed to replace their roof. (adverb of definite frequency)
8  Push the stones down _____ to make sure they stay in place. (adverb of manner)

**B  Complete the information using the correct adverb from the box.**

> already   carefully   consequently   currently   economically   eventually   globally   there

Babcock Ranch may become the first solar-powered community in the United States. Its developer, Syd Kitson, has been **1** _____ planning a sustainable community that will act as a model for other towns **2** _____. The community's residents will live in homes with solar heating and energy-saving appliances. **3** _____, it will be cheaper to heat the homes.

Some people have **4** _____ bought homes, but only a few people are **5** _____ living **6** _____. However, Babcock Ranch's developer feels that a town of 50,000 people by 2040 is not unrealistic. Will the community **7** _____ be a model for future cities? Kitson hopes so. "We want to prove that something like this can work **8** _____ so that others will do it," he says.

## ❙ UNIT 5—future perfect

### Function

We use the future perfect to talk about an action or situation that will be completed before a specific time or event in the future.

### Form

| will + have + past participle | Tomorrow I **will have been** at this company for ten years. |
| | I believe that researchers **will have found** a cure for cancer by 2030. |
| will + not + have + past participle | He **won't have finished** the exam before the bell rings. |
| | I predict that we **won't have established** colonies on Mars by 2050. |

**A** **Complete the conversations with future perfect form of the verbs in parentheses.**

**1** A: Do you think humans will colonize Mars someday?
 B: Sure. I mean, someday. I'd guess we **1** _____ (colonize) Mars by around 2030. Of course, we **2** _____ (make) a lot of trips back and forth before then.
 A: I don't think we **3** _____ (establish) colonies there that early, but maybe around 2050 or so.

**2** A: Do you think humans will ever do anything about climate change?
 B: Yes, I do. I think that climatologists **4** _____ (deal) with the problem successfully by 2025.
 A: Really? That's not too far away.
 B: I know. I really believe we **5** _____ (reverse) the trend by then.

**3** A: I can't believe you're moving to the suburbs next week.
 B: I know! By this time next week, I **6** _____ (move) out of my apartment. If all goes well, I **7** _____ (ship) all my belongings to my new place by then, too.
 A: Oh, I'm not moving that far away. I'm sure we **8** _____ (get) together a couple of times before then.
 B: Well, I hope to see you again before the end of the year.

**4** A: Have you finished writing your book?
 B: No, not yet. But hopefully in two months' time I **9** _____ (finish) it.
 A: Really? That's impressive! Do you think it will be successful?
 B: I hope so. My publisher says that by 2024 it **10** _____ (sell) a million copies and that we **11** _____ (start) to negotiate a deal with a streaming service.
 A: Well, good luck!

**B** **Complete the sentences with your own predictions. Use the future perfect with *will* or *won't* and the verb in parentheses.**

**1** By 2050, human health _____ (improve) a lot.
**2** Many animal species _____ (disappear) within the next 100 years.
**3** Sea levels _____ (rise) over many coastal cities by 2030.
**4** During my lifetime, doctors _____ (cure) most diseases.
**5** By next year, scientists _____ (make) an exciting new discovery.
**6** By the 22nd century, the population _____ (increase) to dangerous levels.
**7** By 2060, robots _____ (take) the place of human beings in many jobs.
**8** By the end of this decade, I _____ (learn) two more foreign languages.

# UNIT 5—future perfect progressive

## Function

We use the future perfect progressive to talk about a continuous action or situation that will be completed before a specific time or event in the future. Unlike the future perfect simple, the future perfect progressive focuses on the duration of the action.

## Form

| will + have been + verb -ing | Next year, I **will have been living** here for exactly five years. |
| will + not + have been + verb -ing | Unless it gets fixed, this computer **won't have been working** for six months. |

**A** Complete the sentences with the future perfect progressive form of the verbs in parentheses.

1 By next year, she _____ (live) here for 10 years.
2 At 4:00, he _____ (play) tennis for 90 minutes.
3 When Tom finishes the housework, he _____ (clean) for two hours.
4 By 6 p.m., they _____ (practice) the play for an hour.
5 By the time she comes back from New Zealand, Mila _____ (not live) in London for three years.
6 How long _____ you _____ (work) by the time you retire?
7 At the end of this term, we _____ (study) English for 12 weeks.
8 When the store finally opens, we _____ (wait) here for two hours.

**B** Complete the conversations with the future perfect progressive of the verbs from the box. There are two verbs you do not need.

backpack   do   prepare   stay   study   try   wait   work

1 A: Are you worried about your job interview in Paris?
  B: No, not really. When I leave for France, I _____ for it for more than a month.
2 A: How long has Patricia been learning English?
  B: At the end of this course, she _____ English for six years.
3 A: Do you think Matt's team will finish the report in time?
  B: Yes. They _____ on it for nearly three days tomorrow.
4 A: How long are you going to stay in Italy?
  B: On Sunday, we _____ in Tuscany for two weeks and we'd like to stay one more week. There's so much to see!
5 A: How many countries has your sister visited during her journey?
  B: I don't really know. But she _____ around the world for a year before she gets back home.
6 A: I can't believe we still don't have any news about our new contract!
  B: I know! By this evening, we _____ for over eight hours.

## Unit 1

### Track 2

business enterprise     tradespeople
free trade     trade policy
trade barrier

### Track 3

**Speaker 1:** It was always my intention to start up my own business, although I don't think I realized how much of a challenge it would turn out to be. I was living in the US and working in the hospitality industry, but, in 2009, I lost my job. After that, I decided to move back to Mexico City and try and set up my own business. I had a friend I'd known since we were young, and he and I agreed to go into business together. At the time, there were plenty of hostels for backpackers and travelers, as you'd expect I guess, but they were very basic. We imagined something else—a hostel that was really stylish and sophisticated. We thought it would appeal to experienced travelers. We imagined a kind of "traveler hub" with good-quality rooms that also provided other services that experienced travelers want; you know … somewhere to eat, a social area to connect with other people, a rooftop pool, private rather than shared bathrooms, a laundry area … that kind of thing. I convinced my family to give me money and after doing a lot of paperwork, I even managed to get a loan from the bank. Finally, I was able to buy an old building and start turning my ideas into reality. Things went well initially. Then the person I thought was my friend backed out and went to Europe with his girlfriend. That's why I was left to do everything on my own. Somehow, I managed to get the hostel opened in 2012. In the first couple of years, we did really well, and things started to look up. But then people in the neighborhood started renting out their homes through companies like Airbnb and HomeAway, and because of that, our bookings fell dramatically. I don't blame them—what a great way to make money, after all! Interestingly, the neighborhood of Roma Sur where the hostel was located saw a 285% increase in bookings through Airbnb between 2014 and 15. Owing to so much competition, we just couldn't make enough money. The Hostel Roma closed down in 2017.

**Speaker 2:** I think it's true to say that my small business took off due to help—well, due to indirect help—from a multinational bank. I have a mobile food truck and sell Thai street food. For many years, I'd been selling at local markets or music festivals or sometimes on South Beach. You need to have a license to park your truck and sell, and there are limits to how long you can stay in one place. It was putting me off running the business, to be honest, because I didn't have a regular spot, so some days I'd hardly sell anything. Then I got a call from the National Food Truck Association, which is an organization I belong to.

**Speaker 3:** They told me that a big bank had transferred its head office to the outskirts of the city because of rising rental costs and that they wanted to offer their staff a variety of gourmet food from trucks set up in a communal, outdoor space—in addition to a staff cafeteria. And they wanted to know

if I'd like to be part of the project. Well, of course I said yes! So, basically, every Monday and Thursday, I'm there with my chicken satay and my pad thai and stir-fried rice. Business is booming! It's a really cool space, and workers at the bank say they love having such interesting and varied options for lunch. There's a bagel truck and a guy who has different kinds of burgers and a salad truck. Other businesses in the area are interested in getting involved, too, so I might be able to move around during the week to different venues. Because I've cornered the market in Thai food, I'm guaranteed to sell out by the end of the day, and therefore my profits are up by around 50%. It was the most amazing opportunity and one I'm so glad to have been offered.

### Track 4

#### Bitcoin and Blockchain Technology

In recent years, Bitcoin and other cryptocurrencies have become much more common. You can convert regular money into bitcoins online. You can then buy, sell, and invest bitcoins, and you can spend bitcoins at companies such as Microsoft. You can even use bitcoins to pay for a trip into space with Virgin Galactic! But what exactly is Bitcoin and how might the technology it is based on change our world in the future?

Most regular currencies, such as the US dollar, are controlled by a central bank. In the case of the dollar, the Federal Reserve controls the supply of money and generally makes sure there is enough money to meet demand but still maintain the value of the currency. The dollar is only worth something because the Federal Reserve supports the currency. However, Bitcoin is a digital currency without any central control. Its value is created by the blockchain technology behind it.

Bitcoin started in 2008 when an article describing a new digital currency was published under the name of Satoshi Nakamoto. Nakamoto is a mysterious person, and no one knows who he or she is. The following year, 2009, the first bitcoins appeared. Bitcoins are "mined" by computers solving very complicated mathematical problems in the Bitcoin system. For doing this, they are rewarded with bitcoins. Over time, these problems get harder to solve, and so it becomes harder to create bitcoins. This whole process will stop when there are 21 million bitcoins, and no more will be created. But don't think you can get rich easily by mining bitcoins. You need a warehouse full of specialized computers to do the kind of work the system requires.

So how do you spend bitcoins? It's all built around the blockchain. The blockchain is a record of every single transaction involving bitcoins since the currency started. Bitcoins are stored as encrypted strings of characters in digital wallets. When you send a bitcoin from your account to another account, computers on the network start to confirm that transaction. This is the mining work that earns bitcoins. When enough computers have confirmed it, it becomes part of the blockchain, and that bitcoin now belongs to the other person and is stored in their wallet.

Blockchain technology has applications in many other areas where we need to securely track things. For example, it could be used to locate and process all the parts involved in a business's supply chain, making manufacturing more efficient. This would lead to cheaper products. It could be used to create a secure digital voting system. And in a world of "the internet of things"—where devices, such as driverless cars, are connected and share data—blockchain technology can make communication between those devices safe and secure.

Bitcoin could be just the beginning of a data revolution.

## Unit 2

### Track 2

record, record, increase, increase, decrease, decrease, produce, produce, discount, discount, research, research

### Track 3

**Alicia:** OK, so we have to prepare a presentation on inequality in sports for the next class. Let's talk about what the issues are.

**Matt:** I was listening to a podcast about sports funding last night, and they were saying that one of the biggest problems in sports is with inequality in funding, you know, the way in which some sports and athletes get more money than others.

**Alicia:** You mean how much money male players get in comparison to female players? They get so much money in sponsorships from sports companies.

**Matt:** Well, the differences in funding between men's and women's sports is definitely one of the biggest issues. In this country, about 40% of athletes are women, but only about 6 to 8% of sports media shows women's sports.

**Lydia:** But is that because there just isn't demand for women's sports? Would most people rather watch men's sports?

**Matt:** It's kind of a vicious circle. If media organizations are afraid that people won't be interested in women's sports, they don't cover them, but if they don't report on women's sports, people won't get interested in them. Whatever sports the media covers the most are the ones people are going to be most interested in.

**Alicia:** And what about inequality in funding for different types of sports?

**Matt:** Well, in the US, there is no government funding for programs that train athletes for big sports competitions like the Olympics or the World Cup. Most of the funding comes from corporate sponsors and individual donors, so they can spend their money however they want. Most of them give money to the most popular sports.

**Lydia:** And because the US government doesn't allocate money for sports programs, there's also socioeconomic inequality.

**Alicia:** What do you mean?

**Lydia:** A lot of sports, like golf, tennis, and rowing, are expensive. You have to buy expensive equipment and pay to be a member of a club. That means that only people with a lot of money can do those sports.

Alicia: So people who have money can do the sport, but others don't have as much opportunity.

Lydia: Right. People think that in sports, everyone has an equal opportunity, but socioeconomic level has a lot to do with who can be successful in a lot of sports. Whoever says that anyone can have a sports career doesn't understand how the system in this country works.

Alicia: It's not just this country. I think wherever you go, you'll find inequality in sports opportunities. In my country, there usually aren't sports programs in schools, so people have even less opportunity to learn a sport.

Matt: But doesn't your government fund and promote athletic programs? Almost all countries have government funding for sports except the US.

Alicia: Yes, the government pays for the funding of Olympic and World Cup athletes, but it really only makes investments in sports that we tend to be good at, like soccer and track. Also, there's no government funding for sports programs for kids, so lower-income kids can play soccer, or maybe baseball, but it's only kids with money who can get into other types of sports.

Lydia: So I guess no matter what country you're from, inequality in sports is a problem.

Matt: OK, so there seem to be three main issues in sports funding and promotion— gender inequality, inequality in funding for different sports, and socioeconomic inequality. Do we want to talk about all of them or focus on one?

Lydia: I think we should focus on one. Our presentation is only ten minutes, so I don't think we'll have time to talk about all of the issues.

Alicia: I agree. Whichever issue we choose, we need to present all sides of it so the class can discuss it.

Matt: OK, so let's figure out what we want to focus on …

## ▌Track 4

Carly: Have you ever thought about why some sports are considered to be Olympic sports and others aren't?

Andrew: What do you mean?

Carly: Well, squash is a really popular sport, but it's not an Olympic sport. Neither is bowling, and we've all been bowling at some time in our lives, haven't we?

Andrew: True. That is a bit strange.

Carly: So I was looking at how the Olympic Committee decides whether or not a sport will be included in the Olympics, and it's kind of interesting. I always thought the decision was based just on how difficult the sport is and how widely it's played, but that's not true. They also look at things like popularity with the public and gender equality.

Andrew: So, do they consider how many countries participate in the sport?

Carly: Yes, they do, although sometimes I think they don't give enough importance to that. I mean, look at basketball! That's an Olympic sport that all countries can compete in? Basketball is a sport that other countries have a chance to win?

Andrew: I know the US dominates in basketball, but think about it. Maybe having basketball in the Olympics helps promote the sport in other countries. Also, there are other sports in the Olympics that are dominated by other countries. For example, in table tennis, the best players are almost always Chinese. So I think there's a balance. Some countries have an advantage in some sports and some in other sports.

Carly: Hmm. I guess so. Do you think there are any Olympic sports that are outdated or shouldn't be considered as sports?

Andrew: Actually, yeah. I think they need to get rid of rhythmic gymnastics and synchronized swimming. Those are more like artistic shows than sports. If they discontinued those, they could add some new events.

Carly: Like what?

Andrew: I don't know. Maybe some fun stuff like zorbing. You know, the competitors are inside a giant inflatable ball, and they make it move by running inside it.

Carly: Zorbing? People running inside plastic balls? Seriously?

Andrew: Sure, why not?

Carly: Huh. Well, how about dancing? There's dancing in every country, it's physically demanding, and it's really popular with the public. People love watching dance shows on TV. I think, broadly speaking, dancing is a sport.

Andrew: You gotta be kidding. We get rid of rhythmic gymnastics and synchronized swimming and add dancing? No way.

Carly: I thought you were in favor of break dancing as an Olympic sport.

Andrew: I am, but break dancing is completely different from other kinds of dancing. Break dancing is like a kind of gymnastics.

Carly: That's so not true, Andrew. Break dancing is nothing like gymnastics. And I don't think it's internationally popular, is it?

Andrew: Sure it is. It started in the US, but people all over the world do it. And it would be an event that young people would love watching.

Carly: Maybe, but I still think there could be several different types of dances in the category of dance.

Andrew: What about things that are more mentally challenging than physically difficult, like chess, for example?

Carly: I don't think activities like chess would be generally accepted by the public as Olympic events.

Andrew: Hmm … I'm not so sure about that …

## ▌Track 2

Host: Good morning and welcome to this week's edition of Medical Monthly. With me in the studio today is Bethany Fernandez, our health and medical expert. Were there any particular medical advancements or developments that stood out for you this year, Beth?

Beth: Well, I guess in the area of technology, Sue. For example, one aspect of this is biotechnology—where living organisms are used to produce a medical product. So antibiotics, which are drugs you take when you have an illness such as pneumonia, are an example of biotechnology. There've been some interesting developments there. Also, some major advances in pharmaceuticals (or medicines), and also in the development of medical devices and equipment. This ranges from small innovations like bandages for wounds, to larger, more complex technologies like MRI scanning machines, artificial organs, and robotic limbs that replace ones lost through accident or injury. Technology is having an incredible impact on medicine.

Host: But will these technological advances help us live longer? That's the ultimate goal of medical innovation, isn't it? To increase life expectancy above the global average of around 72 years.

Beth: Well, yes and no. Some medical innovations can help us live longer, but much of the innovation is around reshaping public health care as a whole. For example, you might have heard of the internet of things.

Host: Yes, I think so. Is that where smart devices are connected to one another?

Beth: Yes, that's right. Well, there's a move toward creating a similar system for health care. This is where wearable devices, sensors, or apps can allow doctors to monitor a patient's health without them having to go to a clinic or hospital. One such device measures about 2 mm. by 2 mm. and, even though it's tiny, it promises to help physicians check a patient's eating habits and predict conditions such as heart disease or high or low blood pressure.

Host: How? How can it do that?

Beth: Well, it's fitted neatly on your tooth, and sensors on it sense how much salt, sugar, and even alcohol are being consumed. This data is transmitted wirelessly for analysis by the person's doctor. The developers claim that the responsive sensors on the device can be adapted so that it can be worn on the skin, allowing it to have hundreds of other uses.

Host: That really does sound like the stuff of science fiction fantasy!

Beth: Yes, doesn't it? And this is really where medicine starts to get exciting. Now that we can sequence, and even clone, a person's DNA, there are so many more medical possibilities. For example, some medicines can now be adapted to the individual patient so as to treat whatever condition they have. This can be especially useful in cases where patients develop infections easily. It would allow doctors to vaccinate their patients precisely when required. In the case of some types of disease such as cancer or leukemia, scientists are able to manufacture specific white blood cells that are designed to hunt out, attack, and destroy the cancer cells. The hope is, of course, that we can eliminate such diseases completely.

Host: That would be incredible.

Beth: There are still huge numbers of ways that practitioners, the people working in all areas of medicine, hope to continue to improve the health—and the health care—of people across the world. Another advance is the ability to reproduce human skin cells. Scientists can take these cells and create areas of skin tissue using a 3D printer.

**Host:** Really? That's amazing.

**Beth:** Yes. Despite it being in the early stages of development, Israeli scientists at Tel Aviv University have already created a small heart from human tissue. The hope is that in the future, medical teams will be able to reproduce fully functioning organs for operating on transplant patients. This will mean that people no longer have to wait for donated organs such as hearts and lungs from someone else.

**Host:** I've seen something about this in Japan, I think, where they use robots to assist patients with dementia. And what about the use of robotics? You mentioned that at the beginning of the show—I'm really interested in this area.

**Beth:** That's right. One Japanese nursing home is trialing a robot called Pepper who leads exercise classes and a furry seal who interacts with patients when they touch him. The global market for these things is small, but it's expected to grow to about $4 billion by 2035 when a third of Japan's population will be 65 and over.

**Host:** And just a quick note on that for our listeners. You can actually hear more about the impact of robots when we'll be looking at how robots are being used to perform surgery in the next series of the show.

## Track 3

1 Were there any particular medical advancements or developments that stood out for you this year, Beth?
2 For example, one aspect of this is biotechnology—where living organisms are used to produce a medical product.
3 Also, some major advances in pharmaceuticals (or medicines), and also in the development of medical devices and equipment.
4 To increase life expectancy above the global average of around 72 years.
5 Now that we can sequence, and even clone, a person's DNA, there are so many more medical possibilities.
6 There are still huge numbers of ways that practitioners, the people working in all areas of medicine, hope to continue to improve the health—and the health care—of people across the world.

## Track 4

1 pneumonia
2 limb
3 science
4 honor
5 designed

## Track 5

1 We all recognize and accept the importance of staying hydrated. Medical experts recommend that we drink at least eight glasses of water per day in order to stay happy and healthy. So why H$_2$o Water? What distinguishes our water from other bottled water is that our water is naturally filtered and bottled at the source. Do your body a favor and always insist on H$_2$o Water.
2 All superheroes have to be healthy and strong. Milk is an excellent source of many important vitamins and minerals, including calcium, which your bones need to stay strong. So when your mom says to drink your milk, you can safely assume that mom knows what's best for her little hero. Milk—your secret superpower!
3 I'm Becoming My Dad!! I knew this day would come—I'm becoming my dad! The other day, I was at the beach with my kids, and we'd just finished our lunch. They wanted to run straight back to the ocean, but I heard myself saying, "You have to wait half an hour after eating before you can swim again." I recall my dad telling me that when I was a kid, and who am I to reject his advice?
4 Knuckle Cracking—We've Cracked It! The *Medical Myths* team is happy to debunk what your family has been telling you for years. Despite what they say, it is not true that cracking your knuckles leads to arthritis. A California doctor named Donald Unger cracked the knuckles of his left hand at least twice a day but didn't crack the knuckles on his right hand. At the end of the experiment—which lasted 50 years—there was no sign of arthritis in either hand. Myth debunked!

## Track 6

**Speaker 1:** Where I come from—I'm from Colombia—we use a combination of conventional medicines and traditional medicines. Obviously, conventional medicines are most often prescribed by doctors, but many people use herbs and plants in treating common health issues. For example, we use dandelion leaves to make a tea to help stomach pain and an herb called calendula to help with skin problems. I see both types of medicine as equally important. Traditional medicines go back a long way, so I see no reason to not use them.

**Speaker 2:** Traditional Chinese medicine goes back 2,500 years and includes different forms of treatment from massage to acupuncture to Tai Chi. The concepts of disease and illness in China generally differ from those in the West in that they are seen as an imbalance of the elements of the body we call yin and yang. A Chinese doctor will usually look at the tongue and feel the pulse to diagnose what is wrong with a patient. Although it takes a very different approach to that used in Western medicine, I think that the number of people who practice it around the world makes it medically very significant.

**Speaker 3:** I'm a doctor who practices alternative and complementary medicine. This means that I look for alternative solutions such as yoga, meditation, and homeopathy, or natural medicine and methods to treat medical conditions. Sometimes, I only use alternative medicine, but I also use them with more mainstream or conventional medical approaches, too. I see them as going hand in hand. Many scientists and researchers only seem to analyze medical effectiveness from the point of view of treating, or curing, an illness. I like to look at it as healing the "whole person."

**Speaker 4:** I guess you could say I'm very much a believer in the conventional approach to medicine. I use manufactured drugs and scientific inquiry to find ways of improving or maintaining my patients' health. We save millions of lives a year with medications that have taken decades of research to develop, and that is proof enough to me of how effective modern medicine can be.

## Unit 4

## Track 1

Good morning, and thank you all for coming. Today, we're going to be thinking about planned communities. Some cities and communities have existed for a long time and have grown organically over the years. Others are planned, perhaps because of population growth or because of the need to develop the economy in a particular area. And early in the process, the planners need to decide how they're going to lay out the community. Two popular options are the grid pattern and the curvilinear pattern. In making their decision, the planners need to take into account the pros and cons of both patterns.

Should they decide to go for a grid pattern, it will produce the following benefits. A grid pattern is easy to navigate for both local residents and visitors. When this is combined with a street or avenue numbering system, as it is in Manhattan, it's very easy to know where you are at any point. A result of this is that the area is very walkable. Pedestrians are more likely to walk between two points when it's very clear what route to take. That is much better for the environment. A grid system also creates neighborhoods because there is often a mixture of property types. So it's not unusual to find stores, apartments, and restaurants in the same area. Finally, a grid system produces a better public transit system because each location is well connected to everywhere else. Take Washington, DC, for example. It's based on a grid and has a very good public transit system. Had they used a different street layout, it would have been more difficult to design such a good system.

On the other hand, a grid system means there are few open public spaces. Open public spaces help to create a sense of community, but it's hard and expensive to include them in a grid system, which isn't usually very flexible. Second, a grid system can be monotonous or boring. The architecture is very predictable and lacks variety. A final disadvantage of a grid system is that it ignores the shape of the land. Were you to use a grid system in an area with a lot of hills, you would end up with some very steep streets.

A curvilinear design, on the other hand, can be adapted to the local landscape, so it feels more natural. Highways can go around features such as hills, and the designer can easily include parks or small lakes. A result of this is that a curvilinear design tends to be more interesting than a grid design. The straight, often predictable lines of a grid are replaced by unexpected changes in direction and level. Another major advantage of the curvilinear design is that construction costs are often lower. There is less road and sidewalk area, which makes the whole development cheaper to build.

There are a number of negatives, however, with a curvilinear design. First, places are less connected to each other. The route from one place to another can be difficult, or at least not obvious. People are much less likely to walk or cycle in areas with a curvilinear layout. At the same time, this kind of layout makes public transit difficult, so people living in these areas usually rely on automobiles. This often leads to traffic problems.

When they are planning a new community, urban planners need to weigh these pros and cons against each other in order to decide what is important for a particular community. The decisions they make affect the infrastructure of a city and the need to build features such as a subway, underpasses, or tunnels. We'll now go on to consider how this was done in a particular case study.

## ▌Track 2

construct, consume, food, luxury, should, subway, super, tunnel, underpass, wood, would

## ▌Track 4

**Host:** Welcome to the show. Today, I'm joined by Jade Simpson, from the local city planning department, and Thomas Redman, a local resident. We're going to be talking about the development of the downtown area. Now, Jade, I know the local council is planning a modern office development downtown. Is that right?

**Jade:** Yes, that's right. We're planning to demolish the existing buildings, clear the entire area, and create a modern city center for the 21st century. We will create an area of skyscrapers that will attract businesses to the city. It will also mean building more infrastructure in the shape of highways, etc. If we are going to outperform other cities in the local area, we need to change and adapt. Had we thought about this sooner, we wouldn't have faced the economic difficulties we have recently.

**Host:** However, local residents have objected to the plans. Thomas, you're a member of the residents' group that is fighting these plans.

**Thomas:** Yes. We believe that it's important to bring businesses to the city, but we feel this is the wrong way to go about it. The historic center of the city is one of the things that attracts investors. They welcome the opportunity to associate their company with tradition and with history. We shouldn't undo the work that people in our city did in the past. Instead of replacing the historic buildings with, frankly, ugly glass and steel skyscrapers, we should be creating new office buildings that fit in with the existing buildings.

**Host:** What about the infrastructure necessary for businesses to function in that area? Do you support investment in highways and other development?

**Thomas:** We accept that a certain amount of new infrastructure is necessary. The highway through our city center was built over 50 years ago, and it would not be able to handle an increase in traffic. However, we think construction can be done in a way that doesn't spoil the city skyline.

**Jade:** Of course, I'm aware of these arguments, but funding is the key issue here. The kind of development that you are suggesting would be expensive and take considerable time, since we would have to work around the existing buildings.

**Host:** How do you respond to that point, Thomas? Is cost an important consideration?

**Thomas:** We need to take cost into consideration, but we don't think it should be the most important factor. The quality of life for local residents would be seriously affected by this development. The majority of residents say that the appearance of the downtown area is very important to them. Most of them dislike the appearance of modern skyscrapers. They don't want to lose the traditional buildings.

**Jade:** That hasn't been what we've found in our research. We found that residents actually would welcome increased investment from businesses, with the employment opportunities that brings. The appearance of the area doesn't seem to be very high on people's list of priorities.

**Thomas:** There's no doubt that job opportunities are vital for this area, but there's no reason to make the city a less attractive place to live in. I think it's a question of the kind of investment we wish to attract. The kind of development you're describing tends to attract large corporations, which could harm local business. What this city needs are more opportunities for leisure activities, such as restaurants.

**Jade:** I'm afraid that creating opportunities for a few more restaurants to open in the city center will not provide the kind of large-scale investment that this city needs.

**Host:** Jade, Thomas, thanks very much for joining us today. I'm sure this is an argument that will continue …

## Unit 5

## ▌Track 2

**Steve:** Welcome to The Hidden Planet, the weekly podcast on which we explore the unknown territories of the Earth and discover its hidden secrets. I'm Steve Nova, and with me as always is Tom Ridek.

**Tom:** Congratulations, Steve! Ten years, huh?

**Steve:** I know. That's difficult to believe, right? For any new listeners, next week is our anniversary. Next Thursday, Tom and I will have been making this podcast for 10 years! Incredible! So, Tom, what are we discussing today?

**Tom:** Today, we're looking at some of the key resources needed in the world and where exactly we're going to find those resources. Arguably, the resources that we'll need most in the future are minerals and precious metals for the world's technology.

**Steve:** But why is that a problem?

**Tom:** The problem is that the Earth is running out of minerals and precious metals, and some, like gold and silver, are in very short supply. Apparently, we'll have run out of our supply of gold by as early as 2050, according to some experts. The production of the environmentally friendly technology we need for a cleaner future, such as solar

panels, depends on gold and silver. But there is good news—the solution is lying at the bottom of the ocean.

**Steve:** Good, because we like to look at solutions on this show. So, tell me more.

**Tom:** As we all know, so much of the ocean has not been explored. In fact, almost 80% of the ocean is a complete mystery to us. And the idea of mining minerals from the deep ocean floor is a very new one. However, what we do know is that there are large deposits of metals and minerals known as sulfides, which contain what we need for our solar panels. In sulfides, we find the source of copper, zinc, lead, and most importantly, gold and silver …

**Steve:** … which we can use to make solar panels! Amazing! But that isn't all we find in the ocean, is it?

**Tom:** Absolutely not. We can get medicine, too!

**Steve:** For thousands of years, humans have looked for medicine all over the Earth, and we still have diseases. That means we need new sources of medicine. Luckily, in the ocean, there are animals and plants that can give us the chemicals we need to produce medicine. An excellent example of this is halichondrin B, which is found in marine sponges. Scientists discovered that halichondrin B could be used to create drugs to help fight cancer! It's incredible! By the end of this year, these drugs will have been helping cancer patients for over 10 years. Another 10-year anniversary!

**Tom:** Of course, minerals and medicine are not the only resources we need. Honestly, we humans need a lot of resources for our survival. Probably, the most obvious one is sustainable food.

**Steve:** Yes, producing enough food for the world is a serious issue.

**Tom:** Possibly the biggest problem with producing food sustainably is that we need to use another important resource: water. All forms of producing food rely on fresh water. Unfortunately, some of the countries that need food the most are the same countries that do not have enough fresh water. So, what if I told you, Steve, that there was a farm producing thousands of tons of fruits and vegetables that don't need to use any fresh water?

**Steve:** I'd say that was impossible!

**Tom:** But you also know discovering the impossible is what we do on The Hidden Planet! So, let me tell you about Sundrop Farms, a high-tech farm which produces fruits and vegetables in a desert in South Australia. Almost all of the electricity it uses is generated through solar power. Because it's in the desert, there isn't any soil, so the farm uses coconut shells to grow its fruits and vegetables. Also, the farm doesn't use any pesticides—the chemicals that are used to kill insects. Every year since 2016, the farm has produced something like 15,000 tons of tomatoes a year, which is around 15% of the Australian tomato market. And all of this without using a drop of fresh water!

**Steve:** Amazing. So how does it work?

**Tom:** Again, we turn to the ocean for the solution. The farm uses solar power to heat up seawater and remove the salt. Then, that pure water, combined with the nutrients from the coconut shells, is used to feed the plants. Sundrop Farms also built pilot farms in Portugal and Tennessee, and in the future, it wants to build more farms in Europe and North America. And if it works in Australia, Europe, and North America, it can work anywhere! What if we create farms like this in all the countries that need food but don't have fresh water? We will have found the ultimate way to produce the food the world needs!

**Steve:** What a great way to end the show! Please join Tom and me next week when …

## Track 3

1 That's difficult to believe, right?
2 But why is that a problem?
3 But that isn't all we find in the ocean, is it?
4 That means we need new sources of medicine.
5 I'd say that was impossible!

## Track 4

frankly, apparently, honestly, arguably, optimistically, realistically, admittedly, negatively

## Track 5

### Trends in Population in the 21st Century

There are a number of trends that show that by the late 21st century, some very important demographic changes will have taken place. The overall trend in world population is growth. According to the World Bank, world population is growing at about 1.1% annually, which means that the population increases by about 83 million people every year. The percentage of growth is less than it was in the 1960s, but because world population is now over seven billion, the population increase in actual numbers is greater than ever before. The vast majority of population growth is happening in developing countries. This means that countries that may already experience a lack of food, fresh water, educational opportunities, and job opportunities will have even more problems in the future. They may not have the ability to survive if they do not get help. To what extent other countries have the obligation to help developing countries will become an even more urgent question as populations increase.

Demographers predict the opposite problem for some countries. They say that the populations of Germany, Italy, Japan, Russia, and South Korea will have decreased greatly by the end of this century. Other countries that are currently growing, like the US, Canada, Australia, and France, will stop growing by the end of the century if there are not many new immigrants to those countries.

Other trends predicted by demographers also raise important questions:

1 An increasingly older population in developed countries. This will mean that there are fewer people in the workforce and more people using social services for the elderly. Will there be a need to raise taxes to help pay for those social services?
2 More working women. This means that women and families will have a chance to be more economically secure, but it also means that more people will be competing for fewer jobs as technology replaces humans in the workplace. How will enough jobs be created for everyone?
3 More people will be living alone. Because of the very large older population, many elderly people will live alone after a spouse dies. Also, young people are increasingly mobile and often live alone when they move to a new city. What kinds of problems might this cause in housing and mental health?
4 There will be much larger urban populations and smaller rural populations because of a change from agriculture-based to technology-based economies. What kinds of problems will this cause for cities, and how will we produce enough food if there is less agriculture?

Many of these issues already exist, and they will become more important as populations grow and change. We have a responsibility to think about the questions and possible solutions now. If we don't make an attempt to prepare for the future, we will have bigger problems than we have now.

## Track 6

**Speaker 1:** I think the major problem in my country related to population change is scarcity of resources, especially water, partly caused by population growth. Worldwide average annual population growth is 1.1%, but, in my country, it's 3.3%. With a current population of 43 million, the projection is that 30 years from now, the population will have more than doubled to 110 million. There is already water scarcity, and it will have reached crisis level in just a few years if there is a failure to address it. Without water, people will no longer be able to survive in rural areas, and there will be a mass migration to the cities. By the middle of the century, people will have been moving from the country into the cities for 50 or 60 years, and the urban infrastructure will not be sufficient to support such large populations. City governments will not be able to provide services for so many residents—services like transportation, garbage collection, and hospitals. The result of all of this will be more poverty.

**Speaker 2:** OK, he said that his country has a scarcity of resources, especially water. That means there aren't enough resources. He said that the problem is partly because the population is getting bigger. In 30 years, the population will increase from 43 million to 110 million. He said there is already a lack of water, and it will be an enormous problem a few years from now if they don't do something about it. If there isn't enough water in rural areas, more and more people will move to the cities. By the middle of the century, the cities will not be able to provide public services because there will be too many people living there. There will be more and more poor people.

## Track 7

There is no quick solution to all of these problems, but I'm convinced that one of the most pressing needs is water infrastructure, especially in rural areas. The government has the responsibility to encourage foreign investment in water infrastructure projects. We have a need for rainwater collection systems, irrigation systems, and water purification systems so that people will not have to leave the rural areas and move to the cities. With better water infrastructure, there would be increased employment opportunities in agriculture, and the country would have a greater supply of food.

## Exam Skills

## Unit 1, Track 1

**Mike:** So, what are the pros and cons of having your own business? We could start by talking about independence. I think that's an advantage.

**Anna:** Yes, that's definitely a pro. Having your own business means you are your own boss. You don't have to do what other people tell you and you are free to manage your business as you like. Let's talk about the next point—decision making. I think it's quite similar to being independent. I think it's also a pro.

**Mike:** I see your point, but I also think it would be challenging. If you have your own business, you have all the responsibility and if you make a bad decision, it's your fault. There's nobody else to blame. Would you agree with that?

**Anna:** Yes, you're right. Should we move on to the next point? How about making profits? I think that's both an advantage and a disadvantage. If you have a successful business, then you can keep all the profits. But not all businesses are successful!

**Mike:** I completely agree with you. It's related to decision making, actually. If you make bad decisions, then your profits won't be good. It really depends. Do you have anything else to say about profits?

**Anna:** Well, you also need to remember costs. Having your own business means you are responsible for all costs, so that also has an impact on profits. I agree that it depends. And it's also related to the final point, risk taking. You need to be careful about what risks you take in order to stay profitable. Do you have any other ideas?

**Mike:** I think all of these points can be both pros and cons to be honest. These are all things that you need to pay attention to when you run your business. Anything can become a disadvantage if you do it badly!

**Anna:** Yes, I think you're right.

## Unit 1, Track 2

That's an interesting question. First of all, I would say that in a society without cash, it would be easier to travel internationally. This is because there would be no need to change currency and you could just use your credit card or phone to pay. I would also add that banks and businesses would save money as they wouldn't have to pay for safe storage or movement of cash. Finally, it's important to note that there would probably be less crime and fraud. For example, criminals would not be able to move money very easily in a cashless society as there would be a digital record of everything.

Macmillan Education Limited
4 Crinan Street
London N1 9XW

Companies and representatives throughout the world

*Speak Your Mind* Level 5A Student's Book ISBN 978-1-38003-158-7
*Speak Your Mind* Level 5A Student's Book + access to Student's
App, Digital Student's Book and Digital Workbook Pack
ISBN 978-1-38003-714-5
*Speak Your Mind* Level 5A Student's Book + access to Student's
App and Digital Student's Book Pack ISBN Pack 978-1-38003-716-9

Designed by QBS Learning
Illustrated by QBS Learning p. 51(b); Rob Schuster Illustration and
Design p. 51(t); Ismael Vazquez p. 47.
Original cover design by therestless.co.uk
Cover adaptation by Roberto Martinez
Cover illustration/photograph by **Getty Images**/Chatuporn
Sornlampoo/EyeEm (background); **Shutterstock**/leungchopan (lower
body), Shutterstock/Phongphan (window), Shutterstock/Roman
Samborskyi (upper body).
Picture research by Emily Taylor

Authors' acknowledgements
Mickey, Jo and Steve would like to thank everyone at Macmillan
Education and RedNova Learning who have made this project
possible and who have gone the extra mile (literally!) to meet up,
work together, and throw around a million ideas, some of which
even made their way into the books! Jo and Steve would also like to
thank Scout for her patience and understanding and for letting her
parents get on with it when they needed to! The publishers would
like to thank all the teachers that piloted and reviewed the series.

The authors and publishers would like to thank the following for
permission to reproduce their photographs:
**Alamy**/Amy Lv p. 42(2), Alamy/ Tim Ayers p. 50, Alamy/Cultura
Creative Ltd p. 41, Alamy/Imageplotter News and Sports p. 52(tm),
Alamy/Ink Drop p. 46(bl), Alamy/Nestign p. 46(tl), Alamy Images/
PCN Photography p. 28(tl), Alamy/Gregg Vignal p. 18; **Jean Marc
Cote**/"France in XXI Century, Electric Scrubbing" Jean-Marc Cote,
1899. This photographic reproduction obtained from Wikimedia
Commons and reproduced under creative commons licence: CC0
1.0 58(tl); **Getty Images** pp. 34(1), Getty Images/AFP pp. 37, Getty
Images/Andresr p. 28(bmr), Getty Images/Cultura RF p. 25, Getty
Images/Dszc p. 48, Getty Images/EyeEm p. 13(bl), Getty Images/
EyeEm/DANKO N p. 13(br), Getty Images/EyeEm/Classen Rafael
10(1), Getty Images/EyeEm/Wahyu Noviansyah p. 8–9, Getty
Images/Drazen pp. 55, 134, Getty Images/Natalia Fedosenko/
TASS p. 28(tmr), Getty Images/Glowimages p. 52(tr), Getty Images/
Gorodenkoff p. 22, Getty Images/Guang Niu p. 28(br), Getty
Images/Hero Images pp. 28(bml), Getty Images/Isitsharp p. 20–21,
Getty Images/iStockphoto pp. 10(3), 12, 13(tm), 31, 36, 40(cl), 54,
56–57, 130, Getty Images/Kevinjeon00 p. 13(tl, bm), Getty Images/
Magone p. 13(tr), Getty Images/Zoran Mircetic p. 60(tr), Getty
Images/Flavia Morlachetti p. 10(2), Getty Images/Skynesher
pp. 20–21, Getty Images/Tim Tadder p. 29, Getty Images/Tetra
images RF, Getty Images/Tribune News Service p. 39(tr), Getty
Images/Visual China Group p. 28(tml), Getty Images/Paul Zhang
p. 42(1); **Shutterstock** pp. 39(bl), 49, 60(bl, br), Shutterstock/
Apichon_tee p. 67, Shutterstock/Arthimedes p. 64, Shutterstock/
Dimedrol68 p. 24, Shutterstock/Givaga p. 10(cr), Shutterstock/
Gorodenkoff p. 44–45, Shutterstock/Kaspars Grinvalds p. 28(br),
Shutterstock/Jiri Hera p. 41(bm), Shutterstock/Homydesign
p. 13(tr), Shutterstock/Ktsdesign p. 60(tl), Shutterstock/Kuruneko
p. 8-9, Shutterstock/Kzenon p. 28(tr), Shutterstock/Lamyai p. 131,
Shutterstock/LightField Studios p. 40(cr), Shutterstock/Lioriki
p. 52(tl), Shutterstock/Microgen p. 28(bl), Shutterstock/Mila
Supinskaya Glashchenko p. 30, Shutterstock/Monkey Business
Images p. 6, Shutterstock/Wit Olszewski p. 16, Shutterstock/
PopTika p. 32-33, Shutterstock/Rawpixel.com p. 34(3),
Shutterstock/Nestor Rizhniak p. 42(3), Shutterstock/Stewart
Scott p. 63, Shutterstock/Iaremenko Sergii p. 17, Shutterstock/
Ljupco Smokovski p. 66, Shutterstock/Supat Toadithep p. 34(2),
Shutterstock/Wavebreakmedia p. 34 (4); **Villemard**/"France in XXI
Century, School," Jean-Marc Cote/Villemard, 1901–1910. This
photographic reproduction obtained from Wikimedia Commons and
reproduced under creative commons licence: CC0 1.0. p. 58(tm).
Villemard/"France in XXI Century, _Barber," Villemard, 1910. This
photographic reproduction obtained from Wikimedia Commons and
reproduced under creative commons licence: CC0 1.0. p. 58(tr).

Additional Sources:
p. 41, "Do You Inherit The Ability To Roll Your Tongue?" by Claudia
Hammond, 30 January 2018, BBC website. p. 43, "10 Flu Myths,"
Harvard Medical School website, 12 November 2018, Harvard
Health publishing.

The inclusion of any specific companies, commercial products, trade
names or otherwise does not constitute or imply its endorsement or
recommendation by Macmillan Education Limited.

Printed and bound in Argentina

2021
5